B-17 FLYING FORTRESS

Walter J. Boyne Military Aircraft Series

F-22 Raptor
America's Next Lethal War Machine
STEVE PACE

B-1 Lancer
The Most Complicated Warplane Ever Developed
DENNIS R. JENKINS

B-24 Liberator
Rugged but Right
FREDERICK A. JOHNSEN

B-2 Spirit
The Most Capable War Machine on the Planet
STEVE PACE

F/A-18 Hornet
A Navy Success Story
DENNIS R. JENKINS

B-17 Flying Fortress
The Symbol of Second World War Air Power
FREDERICK A. JOHNSEN

F-105 Thunderchief
Workhorse of the Vietnam War
DENNIS R. JENKINS

B-47 Stratojet
Boeing's Brilliant Bomber
JAN TEGLER

B-17 FLYING FORTRESS

The Symbol of Second World War Air Power

Frederick A. Johnsen

McGraw-Hill

New York San Francisco Washington, D.C. Auckland Bogotá
Caracas Lisbon London Madrid Mexico City Milan
Montreal New Delhi San Juan Singapore
Sydney Tokyo Toronto

Library of Congress Cataloging-in-Publication Data

Johnsen, Frederick A.
    B-17 Flying Fortress : the symbol of Second World War air power /
Frederick A. Johnsen.
        p.   cm.
    Includes index.
    ISBN 0-07-134445-4
    1. B-17 bomber.   2. World War, 1939–1945—Aerial operations,
American.   I. Title.
UG1242.B6 J5997 2000
623.7'463—dc21   99-059941
                                                                              CIP

McGraw-Hill
A Division of The McGraw·Hill Companies

1 2 3 4 5 6 7 8 9 0   QK/QK   0 9 8 7 6 5 4 3 2 1 0

ISBN 0-07-134445-4

*The sponsoring editor for this book was Shelley Ingram Carr, the editing
supervisor was Caroline Levine, and the production supervisor was Sherri
Souffrance. It was set in Utopia by North Market Street Graphics.*

Printed and bound by Quebecor/Kingsport.

 This book is printed on recycled, acid-free paper containing a
minimum of 50% recycled, de-inked fiber.

McGraw-Hill books are available at special quantity discounts to use as
premiums and sales promotions, or for use in corporate training programs.
For more information, please write to the Director of Special Sales,
McGraw-Hill, 11 West 19 Street, New York, NY 10011. Or contact your
local bookstore.

For Sharon. Here's to our own Cabin in the Sky.

CONTENTS

FOREWORD   xi

PREFACE   xiii

1. Staking a Claim to the Sky: The Air Corps and Strategic Bombardment   1

Selling the Concept   6

Europe: Center Stage   11

2. By Design: Evolution of the Flying Fortress   15

Model by Model   15

Fortress Design Analyzed   33

Tail Strengthening   37

Bessie the Bomber Visited Training Bases   42

Four Engines Gave Greater Range   44

3. Bombs Away! The Flying Fortress Goes to War   47

Fortresses Against the Rising Sun   47

The Middle East, 1942   55

England, 1942   55

Stopping Submarines Where They Live   61

Bombing Through Overcast   65

Western Europe, 1943   74

The Mediterranean, 1943   83

Crushing German Aviation   84

Europe: The Long Haul, 1944–1945   88

Up from Italy, 1944–1945   95

Fortresses, Food, and Freedom   97

Epilogue   99

4. The Human Element: People Animated the B-17 — 105

SSgt. Richard E. Bowman, Ball Turret Gunner — 105
Jerome Cole, Combat Photographer — 109
Roy Test, Copilot — 113

5. By Example: Arming the Flying Fortress — 117

Marksmen — 117
Before the Ball — 117
Sperry Lower Ball Turret — 119
Dropping the Ball — 121
Sperry Upper Turret — 123
Nose Guns for the F-Model — 125
Taking It on the Chin — 126

6. Other Lands: Foreign Countries Also Flew the Fortress — 137

Axis Fortresses — 139

7. After Victory: B-17s in Postwar Use — 141

Hot Bikini — 141
To Israel — 146
Where's the Fire? — 147

Appendix: Representative Flying Fortress Specifications — 155

INDEX — 157

The McGraw-Hill Companies is pleased to present the **Walter J. Boyne Military Aircraft Series.** The series will feature comprehensive coverage, in words and photos, of the most important military aircraft of our time.

Profiles of aircraft critical to defense superiority in World War II, Korea, Vietnam, the Cold War, the Gulf Wars, and future theaters, detail the technology, engineering, design, missions, and people that give these aircraft their edge. Their origins, the competitions between manufacturers, the glitches and failures and type modifications are presented along with performance data, specifications, and inside stories.

To ensure that quality standards set for this series are met volume after volume, McGraw-Hill is immensely pleased to have Walter J. Boyne on board. In addition to his overall supervision of the series, Walter is contributing a Foreword to each volume that provides the scope and dimension of the featured aircraft.

Walter was selected as editor because of his international preeminence in the field of military aviation and particularly in aviation history. His consuming, lifelong interest in aerospace subjects is combined with an amazing memory for facts and a passion for research. His knowledge of the subject is enhanced by his personal acquaintance with many of the great pilots, designers, and business managers of the industry.

As a Command Pilot in the United States Air Force, Colonel Boyne flew more than 5000 hours in a score of different military and civil aircraft. After his retirement from the Air Force in 1974, he joined the Smithsonian Institution's National Air & Space Museum, where he became Acting Director in 1981 and Director in 1986. Among his accomplishments at the Museum were the conversion of Silver Hill from total disarray to the popular and well-maintained Paul Garber Facility, and the founding of the very successful *Air&Space/Smithsonian* magazine. He was also responsible for the creation of NASM's large, glass-enclosed restaurant facility. After obtaining permission to install IMAX cameras on the Space Shuttle, he supervised the production of two IMAX films. In 1985, he began the formal process that will lead ultimately to the creation of a NASM restoration facility at Dulles Airport in Virginia.

Boyne's professional writing career began in 1962; since that time he has written more than 500 articles and 28 books, primarily on aviation subjects. He is one of the few authors to have had both fiction and nonfiction books on the *New York Times* best seller lists. His books include four novels, two books on the Gulf War, one book on art, and one on automobiles. His books have been published in Canada, Czechoslovakia, England, Germany, Italy, Japan, and Poland. Several have been made into documentary videos, with Boyne acting as host and narrator.

Boyne has acted as consultant to dozens of museums around the world. His clients also include aerospace firms, publishing houses, and television companies. Widely recognized as an expert on aviation and military subjects, he is frequently interviewed on major broadcast and cable networks and is often asked by publishers to review manuscripts and recommend for or against publication.

Colonel Boyne will bring his expertise to bear on this series of books by selecting authors and titles and working closely with the authors during the writing process. He will review completed manuscripts for content, context, and accuracy. His desire is to present well-written, accurate books that will come to be regarded as definitive in their field.

Few warplanes have ever sparked the affectionate regard of the general public as has the Boeing B-17 Flying Fortress. From the first day of its public roll-out in 1935 to air shows around the country today, the Flying Fortress elicits smiles of approval as an icon of the American aviation industry.

Part of this is due to the inherent elegance of the design. The B-17 was and is a good-looking airplane, combining a streamlined shape with the suggestion of massive offensive power. To its outward appearance, it added a combat record second to none, one that is well and truly recorded in the following pages of my friend Fred Johnsen's fine book.

When the first B-17 made its appearance, rolling out into the Seattle sunshine, America was sunk in a depression that seemed endless. The country needed good news, and the gleaming silver monoplane was seen as a symbol of stability and a promise of a brighter future.

It was not seen as what it really was—the culmination of years of engineering investment and experimentation in what was for the Boeing Airplane Company, a colossal gamble. Nor was it seen as the expression of the genius of a small number of Boeing engineers and business leaders, who were willing, quite literally, to bet the company on the success of their design.

The advanced engineering investment began with the Boeing Model 200 Monomail, a single engine monoplane with retractable landing gear. It embodied almost all of the construction techniques that would used in the B-17, including all metal semi-monocoque fuselage and metal skin wings built up with square aluminum tubing truss spars. Only two of the Monomails were built, but they were influential in the design of first the Boeing Model 215 YB-9 Death Angel, a twin engine bomber with similar features, and the very advanced Model 247 twin engine transports.

The Boeing Airplane Company was also developing, in great secrecy, the Army's "Project A" design, which later became the XB-15. The lessons learned in the XB-15's long gestation period were applied to the B-17.

It should be pointed out that Boeing barely recovered its investment on these aircraft. The YB-9 lost out to the Martin B-10 as the standard Air Corps bomber, and the Model 247 lost out to the Douglas DC-2 and DC-3 in the airline market. The XB-15 was an experimental aircraft, and its contract barely covered its cost.

Thus it is all the more remarkable that Boeing's President, Clairemont Egtvedt was willing to back the judgment of his engineers on the viability of the Model 299, the prototype of the B-17 series. The Model 299 was roughly midway between the Model 247 and the XB-15 in size, and embodied many of their design features. It was inherently risky, for while the

Air Corps' request for proposal had called for a "multiengine bomber," this was generally accepted as meaning a "twin-engine" bomber. Putting a four-engine bomber into the competition was a daring move.

The management's willingness to invest an initial $275,000 (an enormous amount of money in 1934!) was based on the skill and vision of such men as Edward C. Wells, who at age 24 became Assistant Project Engineer on the Model 299. Wells was surrounded by men of similar genius, including Monty Monteith, Giff Emery, Bob Minshall, and later, Wellwood Beall, who was at heart also a great salesman.

The Boeing gamble succeeded—but just barely, and not before the company teetered on the brink of financial disaster as it poured more than $600,000 into the project. The reluctance of Congress to see the wisdom in buying the most advanced—instead of the cheapest—bomber almost pushed Boeing into bankruptcy.

The demands of World War II for thousands of B-17s insured the plane's place in history and saved the company. But the success of the B-17 in combat came to mean much more than the fact that it was an effective weapon. That success ratified the company's management, engineering, and work force. It established a climate of confidence that would bring forth a stunning series of designs, including the B-29, B-47, KC-135, and B-52 military aircraft. The same climate would permit Boeing to re-enter the commercial market with the most important jet transport of the century, the Boeing 707. And the combination of confidence and willingness to gamble would lead to such evolutionary successes as the 727, 737, 747, 757, 767, and 777. The combination of these triumphs would be the foundation of the Boeing Company's later success in space projects.

As great as the B-17's contribution to winning World War II was, it was even more important for establishing the Boeing Company as an important, perhaps deciding, factor in the conduct of the Cold War. The defense of the free world depended for decades upon the deterrent shield provided by Boeing B-47s, B-52s, and Minuteman missiles. It is not stretching the point too far to say that the jet transport revolution successfully begun by Boeing has been equally important in preserving the peace.

The B-17 was the right aircraft at the right time; it was the culmination of the long design trial leading back to the Monomail, and it paved the way for the later and far more sophisticated designs that would make Boeing one of the most influential aircraft manufacturers in the world.

Fred Johnsen has captured the essence of the aircraft and its era with a fresh presentation and the insight of a man who knows his subject well. It is a subject well worth knowing!

I t flew into history with an elegance seldom seen in a bombardment aircraft. The Boeing B-17 Flying Fortress, nurtured by the pre-war Air Corps, was the flagship of that service's hopes and dreams. It became the do-or-die tool of strategic bombing proponents. While the Axis powers locked themselves into a battle scenario bereft of true strategic bombers, the United States depended upon the strategic heavies to carry the war to the enemy.

When B-17s migrated to England to inaugurate the daylight bombing offensive against German targets, the British hosts expressed opinions ranging from skepticism whether daylight bombing could be done, to amusement and even occasional indignation over the brashness of the American leaders who insisted it *could* be done.

The air war over Europe was far from a foregone conclusion when the Fortresses arrived in 1942. More than once, staggering attrition forced Eighth Air Force leaders to step back and assess the fight they were waging. They always came back, with changes in target priorities, improvements in escort fighters, and electronic tricks to fool German radars and to dismiss the undercast.

When the last Hamilton-Standard propeller ticked to a halt on the last B-17 returning from the last raid over Europe in 1945, the Allies stood conclusively victorious. Yet it was an ambiguous victory for the proponents of airpower. Early precepts of strategic precision daylight bombing had proven naive and unsupportable: Unescorted bomber formations could not prevail in the hostile skies over Europe; the vaunted Norden bombsight, a remarkable precision tool, could not guarantee bombs would not stray; and a Germany lacking in heavy bombers of its own nonetheless repeatedly proved it could build many outstanding fighters to interfere with American formations. But even before all these lessons had a chance to be interpreted and dissected at war's end, other truths were etched in the churning skies over wartime Europe: The young Americans fliers were brave, dedicated, worthy, innovative, and, yes, overconfident. We can only hope to do as well in meeting our own challenges as they did theirs.

And if the B-17 Flying Fortress was not invulnerable, it was nonetheless hardy. It was the choice of U.S. Army Air Forces leaders. An offhand note in a trip diary written by AAF chief Gen. Henry H. "Hap" Arnold during a 1943 fact-finding visit to the Mediterranean Theater of Operations says it all: "December 12, 1943 . . . Capri beautiful with rainbow overhead. Raining in Naples . . . Found my B-17 sunk to axles in mud. Said goodbye to Spaatz, Cannon, House, Frank. Took Spaatz' B-17 for Tunis." By choice, the chariots of the gods were Flying Fortresses. Interestingly, Boeing had chosen a totem device for its logo of the era. And Boeing's B-17 was the ultimate totem of the Army Air Forces.

While this volume chronicles the model-by-model development and use of the Flying

Fortress, it is energized by anecdotal pieces of the puzzle gleaned from wartime AAF documents: Fortresses equipped with knockout windows in the front windscreen could fly with those windows open in flight to achieve forward vision in icing conditions; the ball turret could be jettisoned to minimize damage on belly landings; trying to stretch range by shutting down two engines was a false economy. The story of the Flying Fortress and its crews and builders is much more than a chronology, and these glimpses into the past breathe life into an era ever farther behind us. Efforts have been made to identify when certain salient modifications showed up on the assembly lines, but the totality of the war effort means some of these changes were also applied to Fortresses already fielded; it is unlikely a completely omniscient view of B-17 evolution will ever embrace all of the changes visited on the more than 12,000 Flying Fortresses built. And even as this volume seeks to clarify information and correct previous errors in the printed history of the Flying Fortress, don't take it as the last word. The last word on the complex times of the B-17 may never be written.

There's a time-honored historical image of Americans as righteous, but reluctant, heroes that probably got its start with Revolutionary War slogans like "Don't Tread on Me," implying a desire to be left alone, but also a willingness to defend oneself and one's country. War has never been a way of life for Americans; we are spring-loaded to prefer peace. The 19th-century Colt sixgun that became another American icon was nicknamed Peacemaker, not warmaker. And even the mighty B-17's moniker, Flying Fortress, alludes to a classic defensive, not offensive, military piece. Perhaps the demonstrated fact that thousands of stoic Americans were willing to take the Flying Fortress into battle against daunting odds helped to ensure the strategic peace of the decades that followed World War II, as the Fortress, in a sense, remained the ultimate defensive weapon, used only when this country was provoked. And if the B-17 crews helped to teach future adversaries a lesson about American resolve, hopefully we all can still learn from the restraint of those brave airmen, and not be seduced by our own power into using it wantonly.

This study of the B-17 and its times owes a lot, to a lot of people; veterans, archivists, airplane buffs, and others—some now deceased—who have helped me to understand this important airplane over many years' time. With apologies for any inadvertent oversights, these include: Max Biegert, Peter M. Bowers, Richard E. Bowman, Harl V. Brackin, Jr., Jerome (Jerry) Cole, Tom Cole (and Boeing public relations), the Confederate Air Force, Harry Friedman, Carl M. Johnsen, Helen F. Johnsen, Kenneth G. Johnsen, Don Keller, Arnold Kolb, Keith Laird, Tony Landis, William T. Larkins, Fred LePage, Dave Menard, Col. Tracy Petersen (USAF, Ret.), Duane Reed (Air Force Academy Special Collections), San Diego Aerospace Museum (and Ray Wagner and the library staff), Bob Sturges (Columbia Airmotive), Roy Test, U.S. Air Force Historical Research Agency, Chris Wenger, and Gordon S. Williams. Abbreviations appearing in captions include AFHRA (Air Force Historical Research Agency); SDAM (San Diego Aerospace Museum); USAF (United States Air Force); or the older AAF (Army Air Forces).

Special thanks to my editor, Shelley Carr, for her unwavering support and enthusiasm for this book and the series to which it belongs.

—FREDERICK A. JOHNSEN

Staking a Claim to the Sky

The Air Corps and Strategic Bombardment

The airplane, a mighty marvel in the early 20th century, was a curiosity that prompted rural Americans to call from farm to farm to alert distant neighbors that an "aeroplane" was flying in their direction. Its passage generated as much interest as Space Shuttle landings did some seven decades later. It navigated in a new dimension and generated thrills, excitement, wonder, satisfaction, and some dread. Flight was a modern Mother Lode; if sea-to-sea Manifest Destiny had been achieved before the dawn of the century, the new frontier was overhead.

Like prospectors who set out for adventure and riches, early aviators accepted the risks and endured hard times just to be part of the movement. Some sought—and achieved—wealth. For others, aviation was much like Mark Twain's description of a mining claim: a hole in the ground with a liar standing in front of it. From flying's earliest days, there all too often *was* a hole, littered with the smoking remains of a failed flight.

The new pioneers of the air, like the Forty-Niners, the mountain men, and other visionaries and misfits before them, sought a freedom that ground-bound mortals only sometimes imagined. General Pershing's punitive expedition into Mexico in 1916, complete with frail Curtiss Jenny biplanes, hinted that airpower was a reconnaissance tool, even as combatants in Europe were ever-sharpening their aircraft to drop bombs and spew bullets. Conventional military establishments—heritage-encrusted armies and navies—protectively downplayed the ability of aviation to be decisive on its own and did what they could to keep flying subordinate to their earthbound battle operations.

If Brig. Gen. Billy Mitchell was the most outspoken proponent of airpower in the United States after World War I, he was not the only flier who harbored such ideas. Educated in battle over the skies of France and counseled by leaders including Maj. Gen. Hugh M. Trenchard, chief of Great Britain's Royal Flying Corps, General Mitchell pronounced bombardment to be the most important element of an air force. He also demonstrated, during the war, the utility of massing airpower under a single leader who was an airman schooled in its applications.[1] These two tenets reinforced each other as bulwarks of U.S. Army Air Corps' rationale for decades. In the 1920s and 1930s, the Air Corps harbored free-thinking

A crowd gathered to watch the unveiling of Boeing's remarkable four-engine Model 299 bomber in 1935 at Boeing Field near Seattle, Washington. Wishbone landing gear forks were changed to single-leg struts beginning with the Y1B-17. *(SDAM.)*

prospectors willing to stake a claim in the sky and grasp the tools of bombardment and concentrated, independent control as the means to achieve their dream of an air force on par with the other branches of service.

Threats to this goal included ground commanders who saw air assets as little more than tactical complements to the war waged by infantry and artillery. The ground commanders' line of thinking frequently called for airpower to be parceled out to protect and serve particular Army units, thereby inadvertently unhinging Mitchell's design for massing airpower. Smaller aircraft with shorter range were especially vulnerable to the covetous eyes of the ground commanders, and the Air Corps for a while took steps to render its fighters incapable of carrying any external stores, including fuel tanks, to preclude their appropriation as ground-attack support aircraft by Army commanders.[2]

One arena appeared most promising as the venue of an independent air force: long-range strategic bombardment. By definition, fast long-range bombers could reach far beyond the probing of any ground force and hence conduct strategic missions independent of localized army activity. To some in the Air Corps after World War I, strategic bombers represented the surest way to define a unique niche for their hoped-for independent air force. To their credit, planners involved with the Air Corps Tactical School envisioned a new kind of airpower that would not merely re-fight World War I but would redefine the next war. The gruesome attrition of 4 years in the trenches of France in World War I could be avoided, the Air Corps planners asserted, by using long-range bombers to reach beyond the front lines, selectively demolishing an enemy's war-making centers to the rear.[3] As the spirit of isolationism grew more vocal in the United States in the 1930s, some criticism could be leveled at strategic bombers for being offensive weapons and not the defenders that a righteously isolationist nation could embrace. The retort from the Air Corps was succinct: Long-range bombers *were* defensive weapons when employed to seek out enemy fleets of ships far out to sea and smite them before they could threaten the sanctity of American shores.

A curious dichotomy affected what Air Corps leaders said and did in the 1930s. The War Department General Staff clearly disapproved development of long-range bombers for strategic purposes, prompting the general, if somewhat specious, acknowledgment that long-range bombers would protect American shores from naval bombardment. And yet, in the Air Corps Tactical School at that very time, instructors promulgated theories of strategic bombardment that flew in the face of War Department guidance.[4]

Even the argument for long-range land-based Air Corps bombers for coastal defense had opponents in the Navy in the 1930s. The Air Corps, like an overconfident teenager, was riling traditional thinkers in the Navy as well as the Army as airpower supporters sought a place at the table. In January 1931, Gen. Douglas MacArthur, Chief of Staff, and Adm. William V. Pratt, Chief of Naval Operations, produced an agreement on the scope of aviation in both services. The accord effectively placed the dividing line for Air Corps activity in coastal defense at the practical limit of land-based aircraft range—a boundary that was sure to creep ever farther out to sea.[5] Bolstered by the MacArthur–Pratt delineation, the Air Corps continued its foray into procurement of long-range aircraft. But the journey would not be without peril. Admiral Pratt retired at the end of June 1933, and by 1938, the Air Corps was expending energy trying to get a dictum reversed that prohibited Air Corps planes from venturing farther than 100 mi from shore.

Accelerated developments of aluminum, cantilever-winged, multiengine bombers outpaced for a while fighter advances to the point where some Air Corps planners in the 1930s believed the supremacy of the strategic bomber was complete. Through its own high speed, high altitude, and defensive guns, the bomber could presumably hold its own against ineffectual enemy fighters. The time was ripe for introduction of the B-17.

Perhaps no aircraft up to that time had been so coveted, so specifically wanted, by the Air Corps as was the B-17. It embodied the whole concept of unescorted high-altitude strategic bombardment. So heady was the concept that the B-17 prompted bomber advocates to declare escorts were unnecessary. This had the doubly damning consequence of leaving B-17s exposed later, when Germany proved it could reach them with interceptors, and leaving American fighter escort aviation in the lurch, with far fewer prewar proponents than the bombers enjoyed. (However naive that concept was in the 1930s, its weaknesses had become evident by the time the Army Air Forces arrived in Europe in 1942. In a 1984 interview, Gen. Curtis LeMay, a key strategic bombardment practitioner, said AAF bombardment leaders knew by 1942 the value of fighter escorts, but the fighters to do the job simply were not available yet. So the men of the Eighth Air Force's bombers initially steeled themselves to face German fighters unescorted if necessary.[6])

Historian Robert T. Finney, who wrote an official history of the Air Corps Tactical School, called the impact of the B-17 on thought at the school "profound," especially when coupled with another thirties invention, the Norden bombsight. Boeing had rightly read the desires of the Air Corps when it conceived the Model 299—later identified as the B-17. From its creation in 1935 onward, the B-17 Flying Fortress was inextricably linked with the very identity of the U.S. Army Air Corps, an identity that was premised on long-range strategic bombardment as a war-winning tool. The Air Corps Tactical School, which trained officers as well as stimulated intellectual, practical, and theoretical discussions inside the service, refined its view of strategic bombardment in the last half of the 1930s to include ways in which a belligerent nation could be brought to defeat by bombing one or more strategic members of its industrial heart. The kernel of the strategic bombing

Using split flaps to enhance takeoff and landing performance, a Y1B-17 nosed into the wind. *(SDAM.)*

campaign that would be employed the following decade against Germany was nurtured in the Air Corps by 1935.

With Army ground commanders coveting airpower as a battlefield accessory even as the Navy tried to assert dominion in the sky over the ocean, long-range strategic bombardment advocates in the Air Corps remained committed to their beliefs in the 1930s. The crash in October 1935 of the Boeing 299 Flying Fortress prototype briefly fanned the fires as opponents of long-range airpower tried to fault the Fortress; another ground mishap of less serious consequences in a service-test Y1B-17 also was seized upon by opponents of the B-17 concept. The War Department decided to buy a large quantity of docile two-engine Douglas B-18s after the 1935 evaluation of the B-18 and the Model 299 Flying Fortress; the Air Corps was able to keep a token purchase of B-17s in the budget.

In December 1936, Air Corps Lt. Col. G. E. Brower gave Gen. Henry H. Arnold, Assistant Chief of the Air Corps, a succinct yet detailed memorandum outlining the battle then in progress to procure B-17s. The Air Corps had been given a budget instruction changing their fiscal year 1938 procurement program from 20 four-engine bombers to 44 two-engine bombers. Lieutenant Colonel Brower told Hap Arnold:

> **Any non-procurement of four engine bombers lays the Air Corps open to just charges of bad faith, particularly from the manufacturers who have been encouraged to sink large sums of money into developments of such models. There are at least two such manufacturers. The**

The hopes of the Air Corps and Boeing nearly disappeared in a whirl of flame and smoke on 30 October 1935 when the Model 299 crashed at Wright Field. But the prototype's performance up to that time had been so promising that the service was able to keep the program alive through the rest of a difficult decade until the possibility of war made procurement of B-17s easier. *(Air Force photo.)*

entire industry would rightfully be completely disgusted with such evidence of lack of plan-
ning, continuity of thought, and integrity of intention . . . To make arbitrary changes without
cogent reasons, involving large sums of money and whole futures of factories, is to forfeit the
cooperation of the aircraft industry in our development.[7]

Brower's memorandum to Hap Arnold predicted:

Large four engine bombers are as certain to appear as larger battleships, steamers, locomotives, or trucks. To pick up again, as we surely sometime must, after abandoning development
for a time, will be very difficult and extremely expensive. In the meantime, any potential adversaries would have progressed so far that we could never again hope to excel them. We have now
our only opportunity to hold a well-won lead.[8]

Brower decried the arguments raised against the Flying Fortress following the prototype's crash and the nose-over of a Y1B-17: "Sensation hunting persons have made much of
the crash of the experimental bomber and the accident to the first service test article," he
said to General Arnold. Brower dismissed both crashes as "slight causes, so readily cor-
rectable . . ." He said the two early Fortress mishaps "cannot possibly cause concern—
compared to the proven performance and excellence of the airplane as a whole."

The lieutenant colonel took up a cause that flight testers have long championed: The
very nature of developmental testing makes new aircraft vulnerable to problems, and this
should not be a de facto reason for terminating a new project. "Many experimental projects
have been shelved because of similar happenings," Brower said, "when it would have been
far wiser, and less expensive in the end, to have continued the development after correct-
ing the defects." He observed: "Relatively minor accidents, causing little attention on

The first Y1B-17 came to rest on its chin at Boeing Field in December 1936. Proponents of the
B-17 said such mishaps were not unusual in a new project of this scope; detractors said it was one
more reason why the Boeing should not be produced. Fortunately—for the world—the B-17 survived this incident to become a mainstay of the wartime Army Air Forces. *(Oliver Phillips collection
via Pacific Northwest Aviation Historical Foundation.)*

smaller types, do of course result in costly repairs on such large airplanes—but parallel happenings in ground and sea vehicles have always raised the same cry, but have never resulted in cessation of progress."[9] Hap Arnold, himself a demonstrated proponent of strategic bombardment, lived and worked in an atmosphere of urgent arguments and pleadings for the preservation and extension of the development of long-range aircraft such as the fledgling B-17, whose future was challenged more than once in the 1930s by the Navy and the War Department.

As the merits and demerits of the Flying Fortress were debated in Congress, the Air Corps was able to fund a customary small run of 13 service-test versions, designated Y1B-17, in 1936. It was the first of these Forts that Air Corps pilot Capt. Stanley Umstead rocked up on its nose at Boeing Field that December, its hot brakes fused from strong application. Crews for the Y1B-17s were carefully screened by an Air Corps that understood the loss of one of the 13 Fortresses could kill the service's entire long-range strategic bombardment program. After Umstead's mishap, which left the Fortress perched tail-high on Boeing Field, the Y1B-17s enjoyed smooth flying and did much to sell the Air Corps' program to the public.

A 14th Y1B-17 was procured for static testing of its strength. Later, even this airframe was completed as a flying aircraft in the parsimonious prewar days when every Fortress counted. By early August 1937, 12 gleaming silver Y1B-17s could be mustered at Langley Field, Virginia, where the Second Bomb Group husbanded the precious Fortresses under the command of Lt. Col. Robert Olds. The pioneer heavy bomb group in the Air Corps had to figure out how best to wage war with the new B-17s, even as they repeatedly flew into the limelight in the late 1930s in an effort to keep the American public favorably aware of their important contributions to national defense.

As the Air Corps tenaciously advocated the B-17, 29 Fortresses were included in the 1938 procurement program, with an additional 11 B-17s for the following year.[10] Hardly war-winning tallies, these peacetime procurements nonetheless kept the flame alive and allowed for evolution of improved models of the Boeing bomber.

A fortuitous assignment put a serious young airman named Curtis E. LeMay in the pioneer B-17 outfit, the Second Bomb Group, in January 1937. LeMay, rated as both a pilot and a navigator, did more than fly the Fortresses of the Second Group at Langley, Virginia. He analyzed them and internalized them by April 1942, when he was given command of the 305th Bomb Group at Muroc Army Air Base in the Mojave Desert north of Los Angeles, then-Colonel LeMay was well-equipped to shape his group, and the B-17, into an effective fighting tool.[11] Under Curtis LeMay's no-nonsense tutelage, a tightly protective combat box formation was devised which maximized the protective field of fire the Fortress gunners could use to inhibit fighter attacks. The usefulness of the Flying Fortress was enhanced by the attentions of the ambitious LeMay.

Selling the Concept

Daylight strategic bombardment was the essence of U.S. Army Air Corps identity, at least in the minds of its persistent advocates, in the years leading up to American involvement in World War II. Popular lore says it was a newspaper reporter's characterization of the B-17 in the 1930s as a "flying fortress," which the Air Force and Boeing subsequently embraced, making it the popular name of the B-17. That nickname, perhaps unwittingly, played into the hands of those who argued that procurement of long-range B-17s was purely defensive; a fortress was the very symbol of defense, not offense.

Boeing designers had two parallel tasks as they evolved the B-17 in 1934 and 1935. First, they had to produce an aircraft that truly offered capabilities worthy of purchase by the Air Corps; second, the manufacturer realized the importance of helping its friends within the service sell the whole strategic bombardment concept to the War Department, to Congress, and to the American public. The 20 August 1935 delivery flight of the very first Fortress, the prototype Boeing Model 299, from the home plant in Seattle, Washington, to Wright Field in Ohio, where it would be evaluated by the Air Corps, was a public relations coup. Test pilot Les Tower, copilot Louis Wait, and a mechanic and an engine specialist made the flight of more than 2000 mi nonstop, averaging 232 mi/h as they retired previous records set by less capable aircraft. They made extensive use of the airplane's autopilot as the bomber cruised at about 12,000 feet. As Tower eased the shiny prototype in for a landing at Wright Field, he was ahead of schedule.[12]

Beginning in 1938, the 13 Y1B-17 service-test Fortresses embarked on carefully planned high-visibility missions. To this day, service commanders weigh the merits of operating a new aircraft in the limelight, where success may garner support, but a mishap could doom an otherwise promising program. In 1938, threats to the survival of strategic bombardment in the United States were so grave that the Air Corps felt compelled to take the chance that exposure of the Flying Fortresses would be beneficial. Hap Arnold, formerly commander of March Field in southern California, had sampled public relations efforts by area movie producers; Arnold understood the value of good press. A story circulated in print in 1938 that suggested the Air Corps had a ban on photographing aircraft like the B-17 in dramatic banking maneuvers, lest the public infer carelessness on the part of Air Corps pilots. (Whether or not this is true, photographs of early B-17s do not seem to dispute it.) During the 1930s, the few B-17s extant were crewed by experienced fliers; it would not do to have an inexperienced aviator cause a mishap in a Fortress at a time when detractors were look-

Even as the Air Corps was grooming the B-17 in the public eye, the larger one-only XB-15 was first flown in 1937. Some Air Corps articles loosely referred to the XB-15 as a "super flying fortress," but it eventually garnered the nickname *Grandpappy* and an elephant logo denoting its final service as a cargo hauler for the Army Air Forces during World War II. *(Air Force.)*

ing for reasons to kill the program. In January 1938, Langley Field's 20th Bomb Squadron notified the editor of the service's official *Air Corps Newsletter:* "For the first time the Squadron has four B-17's in commission at one time. Having all ships in commission emphasizes the shortage of officer personnel in the Squadron, for there are only enough officers available to put three ships in the air with full crews."[13] Only a handful of years later, thousands of Fortresses would be crewed by even more thousands of fliers with less experience than their prewar counterparts, dictated by the urgency of wartime need.

Early in 1938, Colonel Olds used a Y1B-17 to set a new east-to-west transcontinental speed record of 12 hours and 50 minutes. Favorable winds allowed him to shave this time to another new record for the return trip, when he averaged 245 mi/h taking 10 hours and 46 minutes to return to the east coast.

Next came a goodwill flight of a half-dozen Y1B-17s, departing Langley on 15 February 1938, bound for Buenos Aires by way of Miami, Florida, and Lima, Peru. The long distances, accurately navigated by each crew individually, clearly showed the capabilities which only the B-17 could offer at the time. The leg from Miami to Lima spanned 2695 mi of sky mottled with storms, as the six Boeings rose as high as 23,000 ft, skipping over the top of a weather disturbance for 300 mi. Their airspeed cut by headwinds, it was with relief when the B-17 crews reached Lima 15 hours and 32 minutes after departing Miami. It was a remarkable show of capability by powerful Fortresses in the hands of skilled aviators. The final destination, Buenos Aires, was made as a goodwill gesture to honor incoming Argentine President Roberto M. Ortiz.[14] For his role in leading the flight of six B-17s to Argentina, Lt. Col. Robert Olds was presented the Distinguished Flying Cross, indicative of the significance of the flight in the prewar era.[15]

The Air Corps' willingness to work with Hollywood gave the fledgling Fortresses publicity and exposure with Clark Gable in MGM's film *Test Pilot. (SDAM collection.)*

As MGM was wrapping up the flying sequences for *Test Pilot* in early January 1938, the *Air Corps Newsletter* said that the Second Bomb Group at Langley Field "cooperated extensively in the filming of this feature picture. All flying sequences were routine Group training from which additional valuable technique was gained," the Air Corps publication explained, as if to justify the use of the coveted Flying Fortresses in a commercial movie. Shortly after the movie's flying-sequences director, Cullen Tate, returned to California, a flight from the Second Bomb Group followed, arriving at March Field near Riverside to complete the filming. The value of associating B-17s with top-drawer Hollywood celebrities was not lost on the Air Corps in those days of budget battles. The *Newsletter* sounded almost coy as it noted: "With the faithful old B-17's purring sweetly through plenty of footage, and with the 2d Bombardment Group grinning into cameras from all angles, this new movie will no doubt be a source of much interest to Air Corps personnel."[16] The real payoff depended on how much interest the film generated among the general public.

The Air Corps regularly printed news items about the accomplishments of B-17 crews in the late 1930s to show off their favored bomber as it flew pioneer missions that highlighted its capabilities. A 49th Bomb Squadron crew averaged 238 mi/h—almost a record—over a 5-hour, 50-minute flight from Randolph Field, Texas, to Langley Field, Virginia, as reported in January 1938. On 5 January, according to the *Air Corps Newsletter:* "In a B-17 'Flying Fortress' with a full combat crew, Captain Darr H. Alkire, 96th Bombardment Squadron, Langley Field, Va., . . . accomplished a night navigation, bombing, and machine gunnery mission to Maxwell Field, Ala., and return, without landing at Maxwell Field. The bombing was accomplished at 15,000 feet, and all members of the crew fired machine guns."[17]

The handful of Y1B-17s paraded frequently around the country—and the hemisphere—in the late 1930s. This formation over New York City in 1938 paired two American marvels—skyscrapers and Flying Fortresses—for the camera. *(Air Force photo 13829 AC.)*

The B-17s' capabilities were occasionally alluded to, as on 16 May 1937 when Lt. Col. Robert Olds led four Fortresses on "a routine introductory cruise," noted the *Air Corps Newsletter.* The bombers covered 15 states "situated in the industrial heart of the nation," in an 11-hour period, the AAF publication said.[18] And in October, a young Curtis LeMay joined Maj. Caleb V. Haynes and a National Advisory Committee for Aeronautics (NACA) official in racing a B-17 from Wright Field, Ohio, to Langley Field, Virginia, in the brief time of 1 hour and 45 minutes. In 1937, these were feats of distance, speed, and altitude.

Extensive war games played out in May 1938 afforded the Air Corps a stage to tout its capabilities and promote its needs. The scenario of the maneuvers included an imaginary enemy fleet off the Atlantic coast. The Air Corps made the most of this, using the innocent Italian ocean liner *Rex* as a symbol for the enemy fleet. Rapid reconnaissance of the fleet was vital, according to Maj. Gen. Frank M. Andrews, commander of the GHQ (General Headquarters) Air Force, and three B-17s were quickly dispatched on a 1,500-mi mission to find the *Rex* far out to sea on 12 May 1938. Curtis LeMay was lead navigator in B-17 number 80, piloted by Maj. Caleb V. Haynes. In the Fortress's radio room, an announcer and two

War games in 1938 saw at least one Y1B-17 with temporary paints for daytime camouflage consisting of several shades of green and gray upper surfaces and pale blues and grays mingled with some bare patches on the underside. Fortresses were dispatched to airfields in the northeastern United States, including Harrisburg, Pennsylvania, during the 1938 exercises. *(Air Force photo.)*

radio engineers from the National Broadcasting Corporation rode along to instantly broadcast a report of the ocean liner's intercept; reporters were on the passenger manifests of the other two B-17s as well.[19]

Using a radio position report placing the *Rex* some 725 mi east of New York City as the Fortresses took off at 8:30 in the morning, LeMay set up a true heading of 101 degrees as the trio of B-17s roared out to sea at 170 mi/h. Clouds and squalls complicated the navigation problem, but Curtis LeMay's estimated time of arrival (ETA) over the ocean liner of 12:25 P.M. was met, as the NBC crew broadcast the feat back to shore. Various reports placed the *Rex* from 620 to more than 700 mi out in the cold trackless water of the Atlantic at the time of the intercept; regardless of the precise number, the accomplishment was electrifying. The Air Corps proved it could vault over the U.S. Navy and intercept a "hostile" ship at sea, far over the horizon. The Flying Fortresses had stolen the march on the Navy. Maj. George Goddard, an accomplished Air Corps photographer, captured the moment on film, showing a B-17 roaring low over the Italian passenger liner. Maj. V. J. Meloy radioed greetings from his B-17 to Capt. Attilio Frugone of the *Rex,* who promptly invited the Fortress crews to lunch aboard the liner! At 4:30 that afternoon, the triumphant bombers landed at Mitchel Field, New York. Writers sympathetic to the Air Corps called the mission unprecedented.[20]

In the wake of the much-publicized intercept, the Army Chief of Staff verbally limited Air Corps operations to 100 mi offshore; waivers to this dictum ultimately dismantled it.

A sea change occurred by 1939 that made procurement of B-17s—and ultimately other heavy bombers—easier for the Air Corps. Aggressive actions by Germany, Italy, and Japan

The 19th Bomb Group operated this prewar B-17B, first variant to incorporate the basic nose design in use through the B-17E. *(Albert W. James collection.)*

Some of the vintage Y1B-17s received permanent olive drab camouflage and continued to serve in the United States. This example was photographed with maintenance crews of the 20th Bomb Squadron at Langley Field, Virginia, in 1941. *(Mike Leister/Air Mobility Command Museum.)*

led to a rethinking of America's defensive posture to the extent that defense could include aid to overseas allies, while American forces beefed up defense of the Western Hemisphere in the eloquent tradition of the Monroe Doctrine. Long-range bombers subsequently factored in both of these areas. If the United States might no longer be inviolate, then the best defense included elements of a good offense. Orders for B-17s, although still small by later standards, grew between 1939 and 1941 as the Air Corps expanded, enjoying a new emphasis placed on defense by the Roosevelt administration.

Europe: Center Stage

If the battle to keep the B-17 in production had been won, the battles the Fortress would face in combat loomed large by 1941. The Royal Air Force took the first Fortresses into battle on 8 July 1941, sending lightly armed Fortress I (B-17C) models against the German naval base at Wilhelmshaven. Valiant crews could not stave off aggressive fighter attacks that year, and losses mounted. Newer B-17 models with power turrets, already in work, offered a better hope of survival in a very hostile sky. It remained for the United States Army Air Forces to prove the ultimate mettle of the Flying Fortress starting the following year.

Boeing's Plant 2 expansion facilitated Fortress production. The shrouded C-model in the foreground introduced an enlarged ventral "bathtub" gun emplacement. *(Peter M. Bowers collection.)*

Notes

1. Robert T. Finney, *History of the Air Corps Tactical School—1920–1940*, Air Force History and Museums Program, Washington, D.C., 1998.
2. Benjamin S. Kelsey, *The Dragon's Teeth? The Creation of United States Air Power for World War II*, Smithsonian Institution Press, Washington, D.C., 1982.
3. Robert T. Finney, *History of the Air Corps Tactical School—1920–1940*, Air Force History and Museums Program, Washington, D.C., 1998.
4. *Ibid.*
5. Wesley Frank Craven and James Lea Cate, editors, *The Army Air Forces in World War II*, Imprint by the Office of Air Force History, Washington, D.C., 1983.
6. *Strategic Air Warfare*, USAF Warrior Studies, Office of Air Force History, Washington, D.C., 1988.
7. Memo, Lt. Col. G.E. Brower, Air Corps, to General Arnold, Subject: "4 Engine vs. 2 Engine Bomber Procurement," 18 December 1936.
8. *Ibid.*
9. *Ibid.*
10. Wesley Frank Craven and James Lea Cate, editors, *The Army Air Forces in World War II*, Imprint by the Office of Air Force History, Washington, D.C., 1983.
11. *Strategic Air Warfare*, USAF Warrior Studies, Office of Air Force History, Washington, D.C., 1988.
12. *Flying Fortress*, Edward Jablonski, Doubleday, Garden City, N.Y., 1965.
13. "Notes From Air Corps Fields—20th Bombardment Squadron," *Air Corps Newsletter*, Office of the Chief of the Air Corps, War Department, Washington, D.C., 15 January 1938.
14. *Air Corps Newsletter*, Office of the Chief of the Air Corps, War Department, Washington, D.C., 15 February 1938 and 1 March 1938.

15. "Distinguished Flying Cross to Colonel Olds," *Air Corps Newsletter,* Office of the Chief of the Air Corps, War Department, Washington, D.C., 15 May 1938.

16. "Motion Picture Filmed at Langley Field," *Air Corps Newsletter,* Office of the Chief of the Air Corps, War Department, Washington, D.C., 15 January 1938, and "Notes from Air Corps Fields; Langley Field, Va., January 19th," *Air Corps Newsletter,* Office of the Chief of the Air Corps, War Department, Washington, D.C., 1 February 1938.

17. "Notes from Air Corps Fields—20th Bombardment Squadron," *Air Corps Newsletter,* Office of the Chief of the Air Corps, War Department, Washington, D.C., 15 January 1938.

18. *Air Corps Newsletter,* Office of the Chief of the Air Corps, War Department, Washington, D.C., 15 January 1938.

19. *Air Corps Newsletter,* Office of the Chief of the Air Corps, War Department, Washington, D.C., 1 June 1938 and 15 June 1938.

20. *Ibid.*

By Design

Evolution of the Flying Fortress

Model by Model

In a decade of production, the Boeing B-17 Flying Fortress bulked up, evolving from a pencil-slim prototype to an armored warrior with a corresponding gross weight increase of about 11 tons. Along the way, improvements in powerplants, armaments, and aerodynamics warranted a succession of Fortress model designations.

Model 299

The first Flying Fortress was a Boeing-funded prototype, the product of company prognosticating on paper even before the Air Corps indicated an interest in such a project, thereby leading to its construction. As a company airplane, bearing the sequential model number 299, the first Fortress carried civil registration X-13372. Boeing chronicler Peter M. Bowers said the first 299 was not the XB-17; there never was an XB-17, just a company-owned prototype followed by service-test Y1B-17s.[1]

The original 299 (all subsequent B-17 models were variations of the 299 in Boeing nomenclature) owed some of its design philosophy to the innovative 1933 Boeing Model 247 airliner. With the 299, Boeing sized the airframe just right—large enough to carry a competitive bomb load, yet small enough to maintain a performance edge. Boeing boldly put forth its four-engine 299 in response to an Air Corps request for bids on a new bomber type, when prevailing thinking favored twin-engine bombers. The Air Corps' request for proposals only delineated multiengine; it did not mandate using only two engines. And already, service interest in projects like the mammoth four-engine XB-15, which would ride on the same wing as Boeing's successful Model 314 Clipper, gave Boeing the confidence to devise a four-engine competitor in a world of twin-engine bomber designs.

The concept defined not only subsequent Boeing evolutions but came to signify the very soul of the Air Corps. The 299 quickly showed up its twin-engine competitors in the 1935 bomber competitions by virtue of its speed and range while carrying a worthy bomb load. Key to the 299's success was its size, which was not much bigger than the twin-engine bombers of Martin and Douglas. The Fortress could carry the Air Corps' specified bomb load of 2000 lb over long ranges, with the use of extra gas tanks in part of the bomb bay, or the 299 could hoist up to 4800 lb of bombs aloft over shorter ranges—more than the twin-engine competitors could muster.

Unlike thousands of wartime Fortresses powered by Wright engines, the 299 was built around four Pratt and Whitney R-1690 Hornet powerplants. Its constant-speed Hamilton-Standard propellers helped advance the boundaries of engine/propeller sophistication. When it came time to arm the 299, once again pioneering work had already been done by Boeing and the Air Corps, so the 299 mimicked what had already been planned for the still-unflown XB-15. The circular fuselage cross section made it possible to rotate the entire glazed front end so that a smaller ball mounting a single flexible machine gun could be at the top or bottom of the nose, as needed. Provisions were made for four other machine guns, in the waist, belly, and dorsal radio compartment of the 299. All of the guns were manually moved and operated in a time before the invention of viable power turrets.

The broad chord of the 299's wing cast a large shadow. The addition of two more radial engines behind three-bladed propellers added to the impression of the Fortress as an aircraft larger than its contemporaries, whatever the tape measure actually said. If changes would transform the basic look of B-17s to follow, the original 299 nonetheless set the tone.

Y1B-17

The Boeing bomber officially became the B-17 in January 1936, as designated in an Air Corps contract for 13 service-test versions to be called YB-17s. A subsequent nomenclature distinction was made to clarify the funding source for these aircraft, resulting in their

Before World War II launched a housing boom, a Y1B-17 cruised low over a sparsely developed Seattle suburb in the late 1930s. *(Oliver Phillips collection via Pacific Northwest Aviation Historical Foundation.)*

redesignation as Y1B-17s. Air Corps serial numbers 36-149 through 36-161 were given to this batch. The YB-17 contract, though small, established low-rate production and kept the Air Corps'—and Boeing's—hopes alive. Still a far cry from subsequent wartime production rates, the YB-17s were to be delivered starting 10 months after the January contract and then at a rate of only one bomber a month.

While the Y1B-17s strongly resembled the original B-299 prototype, a change of great importance took place under the engine cowlings, where the prototype's aging Pratt and Whitney Hornet engines were replaced with Wright R-1820-39 Cyclone powerplants, which promised more power and greater growth potential. It was an engineering wedding that lasted the life of the Fortress, with upgraded R-1820s pacing B-17 development over the years of production. Other visible changes included single-leg landing gear on the YB-17s instead of the yoke-style gear of the prototype, which was reminiscent of Douglas DC-3 main gear. And according to some reports, the YB-17s were curiously fitted with fabric-covered wing flaps instead of metal as had been used on the first Fortress, and would reappear on later production models.[2] One can only speculate how soon the first fabric flap had to be repaired from gravel damage caused by the YB-17's main wheels.

By May 1936, Boeing's company news publication lauded employees for keeping the YB-17 contract on schedule. "Assembly of the first body is well under way; the second has been started and the third is in the center section jig," the paper reported. Even with necessary jigs and fixtures, the YB-17s were handcrafted in many respects. By that time, Boeing had decided to manufacture fuel tanks for the 13 YB-17s in-house instead of contracting them out to a company in the eastern United States as had first been planned. Spring flooding in the east had already slowed deliveries of some contract items, necessitating construction delays and overtime on Saturdays. Everyone knew how important it was to deliver first-rate YB-17s to the Air Corps to enhance the service's ability to promote further construction of Flying Fortresses, and the Boeing company believed its own workers could deliver quality tanks on time. A lot was riding on the YB-17s, and Boeing raised a YB-17 construction crew of 600 workers in the first 3 months of the contract, with more coming onboard later.[3]

In May 1936, Boeing optimistically predicted the first YB-17 would be ready to fly by the first day of August.[4] In actuality, the first flight of this batch of 13 Fortresses was made on 2 December 1936 by an Air Corps crew. The pilot was Air Corps Boeing plant representative Maj. John Corkille; in the copilot's seat to his right was Capt. Stanley Umstead, the cigar-smoking chief of flight test from Wright Field. The 50-minute flight was largely uneventful.

Third time out for the Y1B-17, on 7 December 1936, Capt. Umstead used the airplane's new disc brakes extensively over protests from the Boeing flight engineer aboard for the flight. Had the gear been left extended after takeoff, the brakes might have cooled more quickly. But Umstead retracted the wheels, and it is lost to posterity whether that action was the final link in the chain of events that saw high temperatures lock brake disks together, unbeknownst to the captain at the controls. Then, still getting used to the temperature-critical R-1820 engines, the crew had to shut down two of the powerplants when they overheated, prompting a quick return to Boeing Field. The landing culminated in a nose-crunching tip-up for the Y1B-17 as the brakes grabbed tight. Damages were actually relatively minor, but the ignominious tail-high stance of the Y1B-17 in the middle of Boeing Field only called attention to the bomber's predicament. Detractors of the Fortress had fresh ammunition for their argument that the B-17 was too complex to be practical (see also Chapter 1). The mishap damage was quickly repaired, and the aircraft took to the skies only 27 days later.[5]

Deliveries of Y1B-17s, tweaked by some Air Corps change orders, paced into the spring and summer of 1937 with the last delivery, of aircraft number 36-161, made to the Air Corps on 4 August. At least four of the service-test batch survived in AAF possession until they were surveyed on the first of November 1943. None of the Y1B-17s ever saw combat.

Y1B-17A

This one-off variant (serial 37-369) fortuitously introduced the turbosupercharger to the Fortress family. Without turbos, the B-17 would not have been able to reach altitudes high enough to permit it to fly over defended targets. The Y1B-17A was created from a 14th static-test airframe that had originally been built only for structural tests on the ground. Its contribution to the growth of the Air Corps strategic bombardment movement was far greater when it became the first turbosupercharged heavy bomber. The effect was compelling. The Y1B-17A could attain 295 mi/h at 25,000 ft, far below its service ceiling of 38,000 ft. The other Y1B-17s could only post 256 mi/h at a middling 14,000 ft. Their service ceiling was about 1.5 mi below that of the lone Y1B-17A![6]

B-17B

An order for 10 B-17Bs (eventually stretched to 39 B-models) kept the Fortress program growing, albeit slowly. Assigned serials were 38-211 through 38-223, 38-258 through 38-270, 38-583 and 38-584, 38-610, and 39-1 through 39-10. The biggest visible change to the Fortress introduced on the B-model was a revised nose cap with a flat bombardier's window in a redesigned webbed frame that supported Plexiglas panes as well as the optically pure glass bomb-aiming window. This superseded a dimpled chin location for the bombardier on previous Fortress models. A slightly enlarged rudder with revised trim tab carried through from the B-17B through the D-model. The fabric covering for the flaps was replaced by aluminum skin. The flaps also increased in span at the expense of aileron span. The B-17B modified exhaust duct paths for the turbosuperchargers on the inboard engines, where the main wheels retracting into the nacelle were a consideration. Henceforth, the inboard engine

The B-17B marched the Fortress series ahead with the introduction of a new bombardier's nose that did away with the sunken chin appearance of earlier Fortresses. *(SDAM.)*

exhaust pipes were routed to the outboard side of each inboard nacelle, around the wheel well, and to the turbosupercharger mounted behind the landing gear on the lower surface of the wing and nacelle. The B-models also incorporated a more standardized instrument and control layout in the cockpit than had been seen on previous Fortresses.

The B-17B first flew on 27 June 1939. At last, an operational production variant of the Fortress was at hand. But with increased operations came headaches in the form of turbo-supercharger problems that for a while grounded all the B-models until a lubrication hurdle could be surmounted. When B-17B production was over, Boeing actually posted a loss on the contract totaling about $468,000.

B-17C

One of the B-models (38-211) operated out of Wright Field as a testbed for evolving armament installations that would grace the next in line, the B-17C. Thirty-eight C-models were built to the specifications of a September 1939 contract. They used serials 40-2042 through 40-2079. The C-models featured flush waist windows instead of the earlier models' blisters, an enlarged ventral "bathtub" gun emplacement, and a less-protruding radio room gun window that was to be slid out of the way to allow firing in open air. Gross weight of the B-17C was up by nearly a ton to a new total of 49,650 lb. Engines of the C-model were R-1820-65s developing 1200 horsepower. Excepting the socket-mounted .30-caliber nose guns, all armament on B-17Cs was standardized at .50-caliber machine guns.

Boeing's favored terrain feature, Mount Rainier, showed substantial areas of bare rock indicating a summer date for this portrait of a B-17C. Ventral "bathtub" gun position, while an improvement over the earlier teardrop gun emplacement there, was still insufficient compared with the ultimate manned ball turret installed during B-17E production. *(Boeing photo via Peter M. Bowers.)*

FINAL ASSEMBLY AREA   B-17C   4-22-41   16297-B

The date of 22 April 1941 seems anachronistic for B-17Cs in the Boeing plant and may depict the refurbishing of C-models for British use as Fortress I, the first model to go to war that year. With bombers shoehorned onto the shop floor, this image would give way to a relentlessly efficient assembly line for wartime Fortresses. *(Boeing via Peter M. Bowers.)*

B-17D

Originally ordered as an additional 42 improved C-models, the changes were substantial enough to warrant a new model letter. B-17Ds bore serial numbers 40-3059 through 40-3100. A visible difference on B-17Ds was the use of cowl flaps, a practice which continued to the end of Fortress production. Boeing had earlier embraced close-fitting engine cowlings based on developments by the National Advisory Committee for Aeronautics (NACA). The NACA won deserved fame for its cowling designs which at once reduced drag while improving engine cooling efficiency. The NACA cowling that inspired American designers in the 1930s had an unregulated exit for airflow.[7] Engines like the Wright Cyclone were proving to require careful temperature control, and the aircraft industry added a refinement to the NACA cowling idea by locating flaps, or gills, at the rear of the cowling. These cowl flaps could be opened or closed to regulate the amount of air escaping, thereby altering engine temperature as needed.

Ordered in 1940, the first B-17D flew in February 1941, less than a year before American involvement in World War II. The D-model design was migrating toward combat effectiveness by incorporating self-sealing gasoline tanks and a 10th crewmember. Yet, when war broke out, the D-models in the Pacific were challenged by Japanese fighters that took advantage of weaknesses in the Fortresses' defensive fields of fire.

B-17E

The B-17E introduced to the Fortress line a huge sweeping dorsal fin leading to a revised vertical fin and rudder as well as new horizontal stabilizers and elevators. At the extreme rear of

Olive and gray B-17D was the last model of the Fortress to use old-style tail surfaces, which became more symmetrical in planform with the introduction of the B-17E. *(Air Force.)*

this new tail, an elongated and enlarged blunt fuselage accommodated a gunner and two .50-caliber weapons. Nor was this the only armament improvement; the E-model was the first Fortress to use power-driven top and belly turrets, each mounting a pair of .50-caliber machine guns. And the B-17E used squared waist window panels that rolled on tracks to open the window for firing the .50-caliber machine gun fitted to each waist position. If B-17Ds fought a game battle in the Pacific with their impoverished hand-held armaments, the E-models used improved gun emplacements to take their toll on Japanese attackers.

Serials assigned to the B-17E were 41-2393 through 41-2669 and 41-9011 through 41-9245.[8] The first flight of a B-17E took place on 5 September 1941. After 112 E-models had been delivered with a difficult-to-operate belly turret, which used a remote sighting station, beginning with the 113th B-17E, the immortal Sperry ball turret was substituted. In the Sperry ball, the gunner was encapsulated by the turret.

Production of B-17Es began in peacetime, but with the backdrop of war in Europe, it was fraught with delays in receiving materials. Frustrated in early attempts to get what was needed to produce E-models on schedule, at one point Boeing actually had to lay off production workers as earlier Fortress models were finished, and the new E-model project stumbled for lack of necessary materials from various vendors.

B-17Es served in the Pacific, eventually supplanted by a few B-17Fs and, in 1943, by a nearly universal switch to B-24s for the war against Japan. The first Eighth Air Force raids against German-held targets on the European continent were made by E-models, while other B-17Es operated in North Africa. The desire to increase the rate of production of B-17s led to an agreement whereby Douglas and the Vega subsidiary of Lockheed would build B-17s under license from Boeing. Production by these companies was to have begun with E-models, but by the time Douglas and Vega were ready to turn out Fortresses, the F-model was in production.

B-17F

The B-17F represented many combat-derived changes over previous models. The F-model Fortress, largely (but not exclusively) sent to fight the European war, is instantly recognizable by its use of a longer Plexiglas nose cap unscribed by any metal ribbing. The B-17F first took to the Seattle sky on 30 May 1942. This example, number 41-24340, remained at Boeing for use in test programs.

Serial numbers for B-17Fs are B-17F-BO (Boeing Seattle production): 41-24340 through 41-24639, 42-5050 through 42-5484, 42-29467 through 42-31031; B-17F-VE (Vega production): 42-5705 through 42-6204; B-17F-DL (Douglas production): 42-2964 through 42-3482. 42-3483–42-3562 assigned to Douglas for B-17F production; may have been redesignated to G-models.

Even as German fighters were pressing head-on attacks against Fortresses, the F-model introduced staggered cheek gun emplacements with reinforced K-4 eyeball socket mounts supporting a single .50-caliber machine gun on either side. The initially flush cheek windows limited how far forward the guns could bear. Later F-models used cheek gun emplacements with K-5 mounts that protruded into the slipstream enough to afford more frontal coverage. Meanwhile, Eighth Air Force B-17Fs often sported an internal tube truss inside the nose to carry the weight of a .50-caliber machine gun that faced directly to the front in a recess built into the upper part of the Plexiglas nosepiece.

B-17G

The hallmark most associated with the B-17G is the Bendix chin turret mounted beneath the Plexiglas nose cap (although a few late-production B-17Fs received chin turrets before the suffix letter was changed to G). Initial confidence in the efficacy of the chin turret against frontal fighter attacks led to the deletion of cheek guns, but they returned during G-model production, staggered opposite from the pattern that had been used on typical B-17F cheek emplacements. To provide

The B-17E premiered many signature wartime B-17 features, including the sweepingly enlarged dorsal fin fitted with a new rudder, altered horizontal stabilizers and elevators, enlarged aft fuselage with tail gun emplacement, and powered upper and lower defensive gun turrets. The aircraft nearest the camera (serial 41-9141) was painted for delivery to Britain but kept by the AAF. This accounts for the camouflage variations, the tricolor fin flash on the tail, and the use of insignia on top of both wings, considerably inboard of traditional American placement. *(Boeing via Peter M. Bowers.)*

waist gunners with some relief from the incredible cold at altitude, enclosed waist windows were introduced during production of B-17Gs. Early versions were heavily ribbed and used K-5 gun mounts with coil springs to balance the weight of the gun. Later, to give waist gunners more room, the windows were staggered from their original locations so that the new location of the right waist window was farther forward, necessitating moving the star insignia on that side of the fuselage aft. Ultimately, a new rounded tail gun emplacement, offering a wider field of fire and less restricted glazing, was introduced in G-model production and at modification centers.

During the production run of the B-17G, camouflage was deleted on the assembly lines and made optional for existing Fortresses and other aircraft. This resulted in a sometimes-motley fleet of olive drab-and-gray B-17Gs beside natural metal G-models, plus aircraft

Wartime view of a B-17F shows the pleasing symmetry of the wing and tail. Waist windows on F-models were not staggered; cheek guns in the nose were. The letter J indicated 390th Bomb Group of the Eighth Air Force. *(Air Force via Jerry Cole.)*

This Boeing-built B-17F aloft for a company portrait lacks features commonly seen on F-models in combat, including an array of cheek and nose gun mounts as well as green paint blotching the leading and trailing edges of the wings and tail to break up the straight-line geometry of the bomber. *(Boeing/Gordon S. Williams.)*

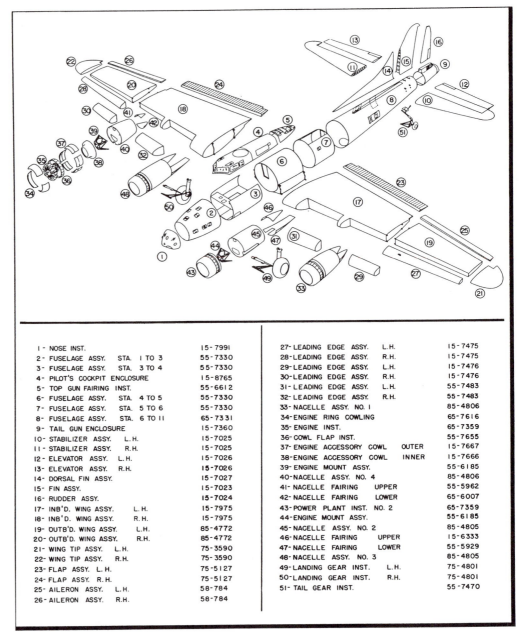

1 - NOSE INST.		15-7991
2 - FUSELAGE ASSY. STA. 1 TO 3		55-7330
3 - FUSELAGE ASSY. STA. 3 TO 4		55-7330
4 - PILOT'S COCKPIT ENCLOSURE		15-8765
5 - TOP GUN FAIRING INST.		55-6612
6 - FUSELAGE ASSY. STA. 4 TO 5		55-7330
7 - FUSELAGE ASSY. STA. 5 TO 6		55-7330
8 - FUSELAGE ASSY. STA. 6 TO 11		65-7331
9 - TAIL GUN ENCLOSURE		15-7360
10 - STABILIZER ASSY. L.H.		15-7025
11 - STABILIZER ASSY. R.H.		15-7025
12 - ELEVATOR ASSY. L.H.		15-7026
13 - ELEVATOR ASSY. R.H.		15-7026
14 - DORSAL FIN ASSY.		15-7027
15 - FIN ASSY.		15-7023
16 - RUDDER ASSY.		15-7024
17 - INB'D. WING ASSY. L.H.		15-7975
18 - INB'D. WING ASSY. R.H.		15-7975
19 - OUTB'D. WING ASSY. L.H.		85-4772
20 - OUTB'D. WING ASSY. R.H.		85-4772
21 - WING TIP ASSY. L.H.		75-3590
22 - WING TIP ASSY. R.H.		75-3590
23 - FLAP ASSY. L.H.		75-5127
24 - FLAP ASSY. R.H.		75-5127
25 - AILERON ASSY. L.H.		58-784
26 - AILERON ASSY. R.H.		58-784

27 - LEADING EDGE ASSY. L.H.		15-7475
28 - LEADING EDGE ASSY. R.H.		15-7475
29 - LEADING EDGE ASSY. L.H.		15-7476
30 - LEADING EDGE ASSY. R.H.		15-7476
31 - LEADING EDGE ASSY. L.H.		55-7483
32 - LEADING EDGE ASSY. R.H.		55-7483
33 - NACELLE ASSY. NO. 1		85-4806
34 - ENGINE RING COWLING		65-7616
35 - ENGINE INST.		65-7359
36 - COWL FLAP INST.		55-7655
37 - ENGINE ACCESSORY COWL OUTER		15-7667
38 - ENGINE ACCESSORY COWL INNER		15-7666
39 - ENGINE MOUNT ASSY.		55-6185
40 - NACELLE ASSY. NO. 4		85-4806
41 - NACELLE FAIRING UPPER		55-5962
42 - NACELLE FAIRING LOWER		65-6007
43 - POWER PLANT INST. NO. 2		65-7359
44 - ENGINE MOUNT ASSY.		55-6185
45 - NACELLE ASSY. NO. 2		85-4805
46 - NACELLE FAIRING UPPER		15-6333
47 - NACELLE FAIRING LOWER		55-5929
48 - NACELLE ASSY. NO. 3		85-4805
49 - LANDING GEAR INST. L.H.		75-4801
50 - LANDING GEAR INST. R.H.		75-4801
51 - TAIL GEAR INST.		55-7470

Figure 3—Subassembly Breakdown B-17F

This exploded drawing shows many components that were riveted and bolted together to make a B-17F. Fuselage section number 6 in the drawing, incorporating the important wing spar carry-through structure, was circular, whereas section 3 was open topped until the canopy was mounted, and section 7 was similarly open at the top until the enclosure for the radio room gun was added. *(From AAF B-17 structural repair manual.)*

with some components painted and others in natural finish depending on supplies from vendors or the availability of parts overseas.

In conformance with the 1943–1944 Winterization Program, B-17Gs were sometimes fitted with front windscreen panels having small "knockout windows" at the outer edges. The knockout windows hinged up and inside the cockpit where they could be secured in

Orderly progression of B-17 fuselages in Seattle shows application of dorsal cockpit covering over existing structure with cutouts for cockpit and radio room. *(Boeing photo.)*

Lockheed-Vega B-17F 42-5886 used late-style astrodome bubble on nose ahead of cockpit and already incorporated cheek gun mounts when this company photo was taken over southern California ridges characteristically cut with firebreak roads. Passengers can be discerned peering from the partially opened left waist hatch. *(Lockheed photo via Tony Landis.)*

Though technically a B-17F-115-BO, Fortress number 42-30631 was used by Boeing in the summer of 1943 to incorporate a number of salient G-model features, including the Bendix chin turret and staggered enclosed waist windows with ribless large windows. *(Boeing/Gordon S. Williams.)*

Like a combat conga line, shiny natural-metal finish B-17Gs made their way from Boeing's Plant 2 to Boeing Field, stopping highway traffic at one point on the route to do so. Deletion of camouflage produced unacceptable sun glare to some crew positions, necessitating patches of olive drab to be painted on the tail gun emplacement as well as portions of the engine cowlings and the nose ahead of the windscreen. *(Boeing photo.)*

the open position by using an attached canvas web strap with a snap fastener. The knockouts provided a measure of forward visibility during icing conditions, and remarkably, they could be opened in flight. Boeing said the knockouts were placed where pressure on the windscreen was relatively low. "No objectionable inrush of air occurs when they are opened," a Boeing technical bulletin advised. "However, a whistling sound results which can be reduced by opening the side windows." The change was introduced on Boeing airplanes beginning with B-17G-15-BO 42-31332. Douglas followed suit, and other conversions may have been made.[9]

By January 1945, the unarmored safety glass knockout windscreens were replaced by weighty[10] armor glass front windscreen panels 1½ in thick, followed by a ¼-in air space and a laminated glass pane inside to provide for the passage of defrosting air. Boeing introduced the armor glass windscreens beginning on B-17G-105-BO 43-39117, Douglas added them with B-17G-70-DL 44-6876, and Vega incorporated the bullet-resistant frontal cockpit glass starting with B-17G-75-VE 44-8698.

Serial numbers assigned to B-17G production were (Boeing): 42-31032 through 42-32116, 42-97058 through 42-97407, 42-102379 through 42-102978, and 43-37509 through 43-39508; (Douglas): 42-3563, 42-37714 through 42-38213, 42-106984 through 42-107233, 44-6001 through 44-7000, and 44-83236 through 44-83885;

(Vega): 42-39758 through 42-40057, 42-97436 through 42-98035, 44-8001 through 44-9000, and 44-85492 through 44-85841.[11]

B-17H (SB-17)

Although the B-17G was the last production model of the Flying Fortress, some B-17s that were converted to carry air-droppable lifeboats were called B-17H. This later changed to SB-17. Lifeboat-carrying Fortresses served in small numbers in the Atlantic and Pacific during the war and on into the early 1950s.

QB-17

The docile B-17 was a ready candidate for droning. Radio controlled mechanical actuators moved throttles as a controller, either on the ground or in another aircraft, flew the empty Fortress. In England during the war, a number of tired F-models were fitted for remote control operation under the designation BQ-7. Wartime BQ-7s took off with the aid of a pilot who then bailed out after an airborne controller took over to guide the explosives-filled BQ-7 to a German target.

A number of B-17Gs were modified as B-17H (later SB-17G) versions to carry lifeboats to be airdropped to mishap victims in the water as depicted in this postwar photograph taken in midrelease. *(Air Force photo.)*

Disappointing results from about a dozen operational uses of BQ-7s prompted discontinuation of the program. After the war, drone Fortresses designated QB-17s, which could be launched and recovered by remote pilots, were used for a variety of risky operations ranging from nuclear blast photography to aerial target.

C-108

Any large airplane is an attractive choice for converting to cargo use, especially in the crush of wartime activity, when available older airframes could be a source of revamped transports. The designation C-108 was applied to several B-17s modified specifically for transport use. Gen. Douglas MacArthur made use of the XC-108 (serial 41-2593), a passenger-carrying variant modified from a B-17E, that retained nose and tail guns. In 1943, the XC-108A, a heavy cargo hauler, was adapted from another B-17E (41-2595).

B-17E converted with a large cargo door became the XC-108A, but the B-24 cargo variant, the C-87, was more widely used in the transport role. *(Bowers collection.)*

The XC-108A was fitted with a large upward-hinging cargo door in the left side of the waist section. When a B-17F (42-6036) received a passenger interior, it was designated the YC-108. Another F-model (42-30190) became the XC-108B when it was modified as a gasoline hauler, a job that ultimately went to a quantity of B-24s modified and designated C-109s.

F-9

In the wartime era, the prefix letter F was used to designate photo reconnaissance aircraft, often modified from other types. Hence, the F-4 and F-5 in World War II parlance were photo recon versions of the P-38 Lightning fighter; the F-7 was a photo-mapping version of the long-ranging B-24; and the nomenclature F-9 designated B-17F- and G-models mounting various mapping camera arrays in the nose, bomb bay, and aft fuselage areas. Occasionally, camera-equipped Fortresses were called FB-17s, and postwar survivors acquired the new reconnaissance designation RB-17G (not to be confused with the wartime use of the prefix letter R to designate any AAF aircraft no longer suitable for its primary operational mission).

XB-38

Lockheed (Vega) used a B-17E (41-2401) to create the only XB-38, a Fortress powered by liquid-cooled Allison V-1710-89 engines. The aircraft was one that had been sent to Lockheed to study as part of Vega's entry into the B-17 manufacturing pool. The Allisons promised a total of 900 more horsepower for the B-38. Discussions about building an Allison-engined Fortress began in March 1942, leading to a contract by July, calling for three prototypes. The silver XB-38 first flew on 19 May 1943. Barely 12 flying hours later, on

The sole XB-38 was a Lockheed Vega venture, modifying B-17E 41-2401 with the installation of liquid-cooled Allison V-1710 engines turning paddle propellers. The promising XB-38 first flew in May 1943; but was lost due to fire less than a month later. The use of Allisons in B-17s was not pursued. *(Lockheed via Tony Landis.)*

Inflight view of the XB-38 shows addition of antiglare paint to inside upper quarters of long nacelles as well as prop spinners. *(Lockheed via Tony Landis.)*

16 June 1943, the XB-38 suffered an inextinguishable engine fire in flight, forcing the test crew to bail out; all but one crewman survived. The loss of the XB-38 came at a time when Allison engines were in great demand for fighters including the P-38, P-39, P-40, and P-63. The XB-38 program withered, and the other two remaining aircraft were never built.[12]

B-40

An idea lingering since before the war, one school of thought in the Air Force said bomber formations could be protected by heavily gunned escorts cruising in the formation. At a

The XB-40 used a Martin top turret in the radio room to boost dorsal firepower on this gunship escort version, while doubling the waist guns and incorporating a redesigned tail gun window and, evident in this photo, a nonstandard partially retractable ball turret. *(Lockheed.)*

time when fighter escorts had not yet been given sufficient range to protect the B-17s on deep strikes, the thought of an escort fighter version of the long-ranging B-17 appealed to some. Such escort fighters would not dogfight enemy fighters, but might keep them at bay by directing withering gunfire from flexible guns where needed.

Accordingly, both the B-24D (as the XB-41) and the B-17F (as the XB- and YB-40) were earmarked for modification into escort gunships. Vega undertook the modification of the XB-40 (41-24341) from a B-17F that had already received a power-boosted tail stinger and a mock-up Bendix chin turret installed at the Cheyenne, Wyoming, modification center. Features of the B-40 included double waist guns; a second dorsal turret, made by Martin instead of Sperry, placed after a truncated dorsal decking near the radio room; ammunition storage in the bomb bay; and most significantly, the remotely operated Bendix turret in the chin location for frontal protection. Long after the B-40 escort idea had wilted, the Bendix chin turret survived as the frontal armament of choice for the B-17G. Nineteen YB-40 service-test variants and four TB-40 trainers were subsequently modified in Oklahoma by Douglas Aircraft Co. Serial numbers of the YB-40s were 42-5732 through 42-5744, 42-5871, 42-5920, 42-5921, 42-5923 through 42-5925, and 42-5927. TB-40s, versions that were converted for training duties before they could be sent overseas because the B-40 program was not working out, carried serial numbers 42-5833, 42-5834, 42-5872, and 42-5926. Some of the overseas YB-40s were subsequently flown back to the United States where they were integrated into the B-17 training pool.[13]

Where typical combat B-17Gs could carry an ammunition load of between 4000 and 5000 rounds, the YB-40 could, for short missions, heft more than 17,000 .50-caliber machine gun bullets. The normal YB-40 load was more than 11,000 rounds.

The XB-40 arrived at the proving grounds at Eglin Field, Florida, on 9 September 1942. Following preliminary work, it returned to Vega before final delivery to the AAF on 17 November. With its extra guns and ammunition, the gunship B-40 missed the 300 mi/h mark by 4 mi/h. Its service ceiling topped out at only 29,400 ft compared to more than 37,000 ft for a B-17F. Between May and August 1943, a dozen YB-40s flew combat escort with the 92d Bomb Group out of Alconbury, England. (A 13th YB-40 crash-landed near Stornaway, Scotland, on the way to England.)[14]

The use of YB-40s in Eighth Air Force combat was closely scrutinized. Operational debut came on a mission to St. Nazaire on 29 May 1943. Eight YB-40s were assigned that day. YB-40 number 42-5741 aborted with problems in the number two engine's turbosupercharger. The remaining seven YB-40s were 42-5742 positioned on the right wing of the leader of the 305th Bomb Group formation; 42-5736 was similarly positioned in the 92d Bomb Group formation; the other six escorts (42-5737, the ailing 42-5741, 42-5744, 42-5740, 42-5739, and 42-5735) were positioned in the low squadron of the second group in the formation, the 92d BG. The 92d BG commander reported that only one fighter challenged the formation that mission. "The attack was head-on in which only the leader's chin turret gunner fired a short burst and missed because the fighter did not press home the attack."[15]

The initial combat trial of the YB-40s was fraught with mechanical failures in the escorts' armaments. All of the Bendix chin turrets functioned well, but the front gun in 12 of the twin waist mounts was inoperative due to feed chute restrictions. The 92d Bomb Group commander reported after the mission: "The charging handles of the tail guns are too weak and four broke." One hydraulically boosted tail mount and waist mount had to be man-handled by their gunners after the boost failed. One Sperry ball turret experienced an electrical failure.[16] (These problems were addressed during a grounding of the YB-40s between 29 May and 15 June.[17])

As the laden YB-40s worked to climb and keep in formation with the regular B-17Fs, the bomber escorts' gas consumption forced all but three of the YB-40s to divert to close-in landing fields upon their return to England. Still, their fuel consumption notwithstanding, the B-40s "had no difficulty maintaining formation with B-17Fs," the 92d Bomb Group commander noted. The bomber escorts used power settings that tended to be 100 rpm higher and 2 in of manifold pressure higher than the regular B-17Fs used, he added.[18]

Brig. Gen. Haywood Hansell, First Bombardment Wing commander, amplified the 92d Bomb Group's initial enthusiasm for the YB-40, saying: "Although the initial operation of the YB-40 was inconclusive it appears to the undersigned that the airplane will be satisfactory and will meet a most important requirement in this theater." General Hansell described the positioning of YB-40s in a B-17 formation, saying the concentration of gunships in the bottom squadron was done because this was the squadron "which has been the most seriously threatened by nose attacks."[19]

On 22 June 1943, 11 YB-40s were placed strategically in a B-17 formation made up of 303d and 379th Bomb Group Fortresses. The bomber escorts spewed a total of 15,240 rounds of ammunition at 19 attacking German fighters, for which claims of three probables and three damaged were made. An after-action report of the mission noted: "It is the belief of many pilots that [the] chin turret's accurate volume of fire turned away many fighters before attacks were pressed home." For their effort, one YB-40 was listed as "missing due to enemy action," while another of the escorts was heavily damaged and diverted to Framlingham on return to England.[20]

By 7 July 1943, the initial luster of the YB-40s was fading. The sole benefit brought to the fray by the bomber escorts appeared to be the Bendix chin turret; the other beefed-up armaments showed little advantage in combat. The 92d Bomb Group assessed YB-40 missions through 4 July 1943 and tallied a mission history:

Date	Target	No. YB-40s	Abortives	Missing	E/A claims
29 May 43	St. Nazaire	8	0	0	0
15 June	LeMans (mission recalled due to weather)	4	0	0	0
22 June	Huls	11	0	1	0
23 June	LeMans (mission recalled before reaching enemy coast)	8	0	0	0
25 June	Hamburg	7	2	0	2 destroyed
					1 damaged
26 June	Paris	5	0	0	2 destroyed
					5 damaged
					1 probable
28 June	St. Nazaire	6	0	0	1 destroyed
					1 damaged
					1 probable
29 June	Paris	2	1	0	0
4 July	Nantes	1	0	0	0
	LeMans	2	0	0	0

SOURCE: Memo, subject: "Report on YB-40 Aircraft," from Col. William M. Reid, Commander, 92d Bomb Group, to Commanding General, VIII Bomber Command, 7 July 1943.

Based on the experience gained in these missions, the 92d Bomb Group commander, Col. William Reid, wrote: "Because the YB-40 carries its weight to the target and back the maximum range with safety from takeoff until recrossing the English coast on return from any mission is six hours, using only wing tanks (1700 gallons). By using one bomb bay tank the range is increased to seven and one half hours." Colonel Reid said the estimated increase in firing power of the 16-gun YB-40 over the B-17F was 20 percent, while the effectiveness of the YB-40 against German fighters was only 10 percent greater than that of a standard B-17F. "It is believed that most of this 10 percent added effectiveness is in the Bendix chin turret," Col. Reid added.[21]

Colonel Reid summarized the desirability of the YB-40 in his 7 July memorandum:

> **It is felt in this Theatre the disadvantage of not carrying a bomb load by the YB-40 overcomes the original purpose of formation protection. Since approximately 75 percent of all attacks are head-on, the added firepower of the YB-40, which is concentrated to the rear, has proven relatively ineffective. It follows that the added weight of the upper Martin turret, twin waist, and tail installation which affect the flying performance of this airplane at high altitude does not warrant these installations in future B-17s. The Bendix chin turret is a good installation and has proven to be much more accurate and effective than conventional B-17 nose guns. Therefore the YB-40 is undesirable in this Theatre.[22]**

Colonel Reid noted one serious potential drawback in the configuration of the YB-40: "There is no satisfactory ditching procedure in this airplane since [the] radio compartment is filled with [the] Martin turret and waist gun windows are crowded with twin waist gun installation." The 92d Bomb Group commander made several recommendations, some of which showed up in B-17G production later. He urged installation of the Bendix chin turret on future B-17s, which was done, and he recommended that B-17 waist windows be staggered instead of directly opposing each other. This also took place well into B-17G production as a means of giving waist gunners more maneuvering room. The colonel also recommended the use of a computing gunsight for the chin turret. Later B-17Gs could accommodate the sophisticated K-13 computing sight.[23]

By 12 July, the First Air Division commander noted that the YB-40 crews were shuffled to different bomb groups for each mission with some logistical problems. The nature of the YB-40 missions was taking a toll on the morale of the bomber escorts' crews. He explained:

> **Experienced combat crew are assigned to these aircraft. They always fly in the most vulnerable positions in a strange formation. It is impossible to ditch the aircraft and almost impossible to abandon it in flight. Present crews realize their days are numbered and feel that they have done their share in testing the equipment. The aircraft cannot maintain formation on three engines due to its weight, and the engines are as vulnerable to head-on attack as [B-17F] Fortress engines.[24]**

By that time, the field service test had been completed.

Even though the B-40 was intended to retain a bombing capability, this could only be accommodated at the expense of ammunition carried. Since bombing was not a *forte* of the YB-40s dispatched to England, the Engineering Division at Wright Field questioned the desirability of designing "an airplane which, possessing no performance superiority, will fly in formation with bombardment airplanes in an effort to augment their already considerable massed fire power, which will be exposed to the same hazards . . . over hostile territory, and which . . . will have no bomb load to deliver." In June 1944, with the P-51 Mustang proving its ability to escort Fortresses and Liberators all the way to Berlin and back, the AAF Materiel, Maintenance, and Distribution office notified Materiel Command at Wright Field that "no requirement for a bombardment escort airplane" existed.[25]

Protection of Flying Fortresses would henceforth be the domain of nimble fighters possessing ever-increasing range, and the B-17's own gunners, better equipped in part because of experiences gained with the YB-40 in combat.

Fortress Design Analyzed

Except for a few alloy steel components such as landing gear, engine mounts, and firewalls, most of the Flying Fortress was a metalworking concoction of 24ST and ST Alclad aluminum. A series of wing rib trusses and skin stiffened on the inside with corrugations contributed to the immense strength of the B-17's wing. Spanning just over 103 ft 9 in, the B-17 was actually smaller in span than the twin-engine Curtiss C-46 Commando transport. The Fortress wing had a noticeable dihedral—positive upsweep—of 4.5 degrees, which, while contributing to inherent stability, was somewhat of a trade-off in terms of lift efficiency.[26] With a broad wing chord, the Fortress wing represented an area of 1,420 sq ft, almost 400 sq ft more area than that of the 110-ft wing on the contemporary B-24 Liberator.

The wing of the B-17 was built in six parts: inboard left and right panels, each carrying two engine nacelles; outboard panels; and wingtips. Only the left aileron had a trim tab, located at the inboard end. The B-17's split flaps were electrically screw operated and could be raised or lowered at an airspeed of up to 126 mi/h. Vents in the wing surface allowed air from the intercooler system to spill out. The intercoolers cooled turbosupercharger air, which increased in temperature as it was compressed as part of the turbosupercharging process.[27]

Crowded nose of an Eighth Air Force B-17F showed use of quilted insulation between fuselage members. Visible tubes formed support framework for added .50-caliber machine gun in the nose in response to a change in German fighter tactics. Flexible stainless steel chute in lower left of photo provided feedway for linked .50-caliber ammunition from storage box to cheek gun. *(Jerry Cole collection.)*

Boeing engineer and vice president Wellwood Beall, generally credited with the design of the Model 314 flying boat which used the wing design of the XB-15, said in a wartime article that the secret to the B-17's legendary stability was its huge empennage. The great dorsal fin introduced with the B-17E produced flying traits that allowed the B-17 to be maneuvered by using ailerons and elevators only, without moving the rudder (although good flying technique still demanded that coordinated turns be made with rudder input, as with most aircraft). Rudder travel was 21 to 22 degrees either side of neutral. The span of the enlarged horizontal tailplane introduced on the B-17E was so huge that the tips of the horizontal stabilizer were almost directly behind the *outboard* engines. The large elevators had a travel range of 23 degrees up and 14 degrees down. The rudder and both elevators included trim tabs.[28]

Fortress landing gear retracted and extended electrically, with both main gear legs operating simultaneously when powered, but individually if the emergency hand-crank system had to be used. The emergency engine hand crank doubled as the landing gear manual extension crank. (This ability led to an air show demonstration performed by the Confederate Air Force organization in which a B-17G simulated battle damage and approached the runway with one main gear up and one down. The Fortress's pilot then skillfully rolled

Drift meter with angled cushioned eyepiece protruded slightly from right side of B-17's nose and aided in solving navigation problems. Three small metal tanks in left of photo are green walk-around oxygen bottles carried by crewmembers when away from their main oxygen source at their battle stations. *(Jerry Cole collection.)*

the length of the runway on the one extended main wheel before adding power and going around the pattern as the other main wheel was extended for landing.)

To accommodate the tail gunner introduced on the B-17E, the entire aft fuselage diameter was increased from the point where its circular cross section joined the forward fuselage section. Ease of manufacture and strength were two reasons influencing Boeing's choice of

Photographed in 1943 to depict breaking through pavement at an English base, this view shows details of a B-17's right main landing gear. *(Jerry Cole collection.)*

a circular cross section for the B-17 fuselage. At its widest, the B-17 fuselage was 90 in across. To carry wing spar loads through the fuselage, four heat-treated square steel tubes were located at bulkheads four and five at either end of the bomb bay.[29] (Boeing favored square tubing in other designs including the successful Model 247 airliner of 1933 and the older 1929 fabric-covered Model 80 biplane trimotor airliner.)

A list of Fortress component weights shows the designers' perpetual tug-of-war with the problem of increasing weight as needed innovations were incorporated into the maturing design. By 1945, armament, including the turrets, armor plate, and armor glass, added more than a ton—2766 lb—to the weight of a Fortress. The rest of the fuselage structure (less equipment and furnishings) weighed only 3498 lb by comparison. Yet nobody would dispute the need for arming the Fortress to keep it viable against the fighters of its era.

Some B-17Es still used old-style bentwood control wheels. Characteristic throttle grips (middle of photo) allowed one-handed grasping of all four levers or of the outboard or inboard pair. This was accomplished by grasping the top two horizontal handles simultaneously for outboard engine control, the center four handles grouped together for all four engines, and the bottom two horizontal handles for inboard engine control. *(Boeing via Peter M. Bowers.)*

B-17F cockpit photo shows new control wheels made of metal dipped in plastic. *(Boeing.)*

Typical combat Fortress cockpit shows use of Honeywell turbosupercharger control box on throttle quadrant forward of throttle levers. *(Bowers collection.)*

Built-up B-17 cockpit training aid showed cockpit systems to students at Kingman Army Airfield, Arizona, when photographed 4 September 1944. *(AFHRA.)*

The quartet of three-blade, solid aluminum, fully feathering Hamilton-Standard propellers and hubs of the wartime B-17 added nearly a ton to the bomber's weight, at 1902 lb. Propeller arc diameter was 11 ft 7 in. Behind each Wright Cyclone engine, aft of the firewall, a 37-gal self-sealing oil tank serviced each powerplant. Boeing calculated that the oil system would function properly in dives up to a maximum angle of 25 degrees.

If the B-17's three 24-volt batteries and auxiliary gasoline powerplant could not start the aircraft's engines, a three-prong receptacle for an external power cart was provided on the lower surface of the fuselage behind the forward entrance door. This device was furnished with an adapter to make it compatible with British two-prong power sources. An emergency brake pressure system protected against loss of main hydraulic power for brakes. The B-17's low-pressure oxygen system was supported by 18 G-1 shatterproof oxygen tanks, each of which could supply the equivalent needs of one crewman at 30,000 ft for 4 hours.[30]

Tail Strengthening

During 1943 wind tunnel tests by the National Advisory Committee for Aeronautics (NACA), engineers learned that the horizontal tail of the B-29 Superfortress, under some high-speed conditions, was subjected to stresses greater than those for which it was designed. This led to a beefing up of the horizontal tails of B-29s as well as B-17s.[31] The silhouette of the horizontal tail of the B-17 is virtually identical to that of the bigger B-29. This often gives the B-17 the appearance of having a large tail, whereas the bigger B-29 appears to have a small horizontal tail.

Boeing test pilot A. Elliott Merrill had a harrowing experience involving complete loss of the horizontal tail on the first B-17F in the skies near Tacoma, Washington. The Fort had

Hinged floor panels in the radio room allowed access to camera well where strike photos were made, as seen in a 390th Bomb Group B-17 being serviced by photo specialist Manny Berger. It was up to the radio operator to switch the automatic K-21 camera on before bomb release and off after. *(Jerry Cole collection.)*

Jerry Cole poked his head from the camera well in a 390th Bomb Group B-17 in England while another technician hefted the strike camera to be installed there. *(Jerry Cole collection.)*

been fitted with extra long-range gasoline tanks in the wings. Euphemistically called "Tokyo tanks," the extra fuel cells were to become standard on B-17F-55-BO and later variants pending successful testing. Merrill's task was to fly the modified B-17F with Tokyo tanks in a series of dives and climbs over Puget Sound in western Washington so that rapid changes in outside air pressure would test the new gas tanks' venting capabilities. In the instrumented B-17F, colored fluid in a bank of manometer tubes rose and fell with pressure changes in the tanks while a motion-picture camera recorded the fluctuations for later analysis.[32]

Merrill later recalled that it was during a 30 degree dive at about 330 mi/h that the fabric covering the elevators pulled loose from the aluminum skeleton and left the airplane. The sudden loss of the elevators placed high stress loads on the horizontal stabilizers, which suddenly and dramatically broke from the fuselage. Up in the pilot's seat, Elliott Merrill was slammed into momentary unconsciousness by the violent pitch-up brought on by the loss of the entire horizontal tail surface. As his life-delivering blood returned to his head, Merrill became aware that the stricken B-17 was running out of airspeed in a too-steep climb. With no elevators to alter its pitching, he was helpless to stop the bomber from starting a tail slide followed by a downward pitching of the nose.

The test crew knew they must leave the broken bomber immediately. After his copilot evacuated the cockpit, Elliott stood up to leave, but his cumbersome parachute impeded his way between the two seats. For an instant, Merrill contemplated the undesirable option of removing the parachute pack before leaving the cockpit and slipping it back on before bailing out. Momentum intervened as the Fortress reached the apex of another climb and then dropped away in a dive, rendering Merrill weightless as he floated over the seats. The movement was over so quickly that Elliott found himself looking out the open bomb bay, hanging on to a bomb rack as he prepared to jump, still not quite sure how he avoided hanging up in the cockpit or on the Sperry top turret structure.

Merrill was free of the Fortress at about 16,000 ft. The elevators had ripped off over sparsely populated Hood Canal, but now, as Elliott watched from his parachute perch, the unmanned B-17F described a huge full circle as it continued to porpoise up in a climb, followed by a nosedive and another climb, losing altitude. A new concern of Elliott's was the possibility the big bomber might head toward the city of Tacoma, Washington. But the bomber ran out of altitude in its wide circuit in the woods near Purdy, Washington, Merrill recalled later. Fascinated by the sight, he saw some of the Fortress' Wright Cyclone engines keep on moving after the aircraft hit, fingers of fire pointing toward the severed powerplants' hiding places in the fir forest.[33]

The drama renewed itself as Elliott Merrill realized his parachute and the crashing B-17 had meandered to the same parcel of real estate, and he could feel heat from the burning wreckage as he yanked on parachute shroud lines in an effort to drift away from the inferno. All six crewmen parachuted safely and trudged to the

A youthfully earnest B-17 radio operator, TSgt. Warren M. Fleener of Sheldon, Missouri, tuned the equipment in a 388th Bomb Group Fortress in England. Dials behind Fleener showed life-giving oxygen pressure and flow. *(Brown/USAFA.)*

A grinning Elliott Merrill (lower right) posed with his Boeing flight test compatriots beside a B-17 after they earned membership in the Caterpillar Club for bailing out of a stricken B-17F over Puget Sound. The caterpillar referred to silk; bailing out was called "hitting the silk." *(Boeing photo.)*

crash site, where the charred bomber appeared to have rendered the risky flight useless. Then, as miraculously as other events of the day, one of the men kicked through the debris and uncovered the camera that had been trained on the manometer boards. The film survived the crash and fire, and yielded its information.

Additionally, the means for attaching B-17 elevator fabric to the ribs was subsequently strengthened, Merrill remembered. Flathead sheet-metal screws were used to provide greater security to the elevator fabric beginning with Boeing B-17F 42-30156 as well as being employed on 42-29964; Douglas and Vega followed suit. Boeing described the problem:

> The change became necessary due to the possibility of loosening of the fabric on the elevator during high velocity dives. In the past the fabric has been held by clip fasteners placed along the chord flanges of the elevator ribs. No attachment has been made along the spars between the ribs. Tests indicated that during high speed dive conditions the fabric tended to balloon slightly between the ribs and in turn loosen the fabric clips.

To keep the fabric from working loose under dive loads, formed channels were placed over the fabric along the elevator ribs, secured by flathead screws, and protected by cloth tape. In an economy of production, the screws occupied holes in the ribs previously made for the fabric attachment clips. This superseded a stop-gap use of tie cords along elevator ribs that was instated when the problem was identified.[34]

In the hectic pace of wartime test and development, a B-17F originally sent out to evaluate fuel tank venting became catastrophic evidence in the evaluation of new ways to attach elevator fabric.

Miss Virginia was a B-17E (41-2539) operated as an airborne gasoline receiver in 1943 tests by the AAF using a B-24 as the tanker. It was a complex, but functional, British-designed system using hoses and grappling hooks to effect a connection between the two bombers in flight. *(AAF via Ralph Hoewing.)*

A B-17E carried two glide bombs in a stateside test. Stubby wings and tail could provide a degree of maneuverability during the descent of the bombs, as monitored and manipulated from the bomber. *(AAF photo.)*

One proposal for retrieving fighters with inoperable engines from continental Europe after the Allied landings in mid-1944 called for towing them back to England for repairs. A stateside test of the concept paired a plucky pilot in a P-47 with a B-17F that snatched the towline held above the ground by poles (not visible in this photo). *(AAF photo.)*

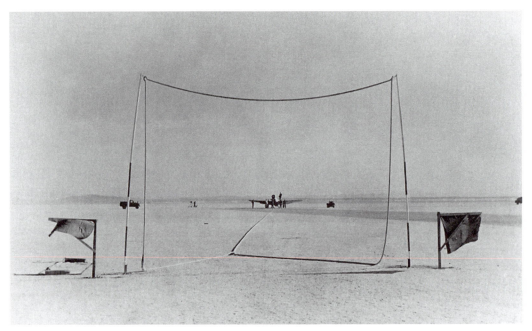

The intended "glider" to be snatched by the testbed B-17 was a propellerless P-51 this time. A long towline led from fighter to poles holding rope aloft so that the B-17 tow plane could engage the line in flight. *(AAF photo.)*

Bessie the Bomber Visited Training Bases

Beginning in January 1943, Boeing's Service Department campaigned a special B-17F, visiting B-17 training bases in Second Air Force to assist with the grooming of Fortress crews for combat. Nicknamed *Bessie,* the Fortress provided by Second Air Force was distinctively

Bessie was a special B-17F operated by Boeing and Second Air Force to bolster the knowledge of new crews ready to head overseas in 1943. Yellow stripes made *Bessie* stand out in the traffic pattern wherever she went. *(Gordon S. Williams collection.)*

In May of 1943, the flight line at Geiger Field, Spokane, Washington, was stocked with brand-new B-17Fs ready to take crews to England as the 390th Bomb Group went to war. This impressive manifestation of the arsenal of democracy was captured on film by Jerome "Jerry" Cole, a young photographer assigned to the group. Visible on the oil-spattered light concrete is the striped *Bessie* B-17 demonstrator. *(Jerry Cole.)*

marked with brilliant chrome-yellow paint stripes—the same color used to denote some training airplanes. Before *Bessie* sallied forth, the top turret was removed to make more room on the enlarged flight deck for student observers. The bomb bay was modified to carry films, books, charts, and diagrams. At training bases, pilots were given instruction on the ground, and in the air, on emergency takeoff and landing procedures, power settings for endurance and range, plus systems lectures by Boeing representatives. A Boeing technical bulletin observed: "Pilots at all of the air bases visited were enthusiastic about the idea because it permitted them to take an airplane, free from ordinary operational schedules, and practice routine flight procedures under the guidance of pilots specializing on the B-17."[35]

In the rush to combat in 1943, *Bessie* gave new fliers a dose of confidence before they began their overseas adventure. *Bessie* was squired by Second Air Force Capt. S.O. Davis and a crew of Boeing technical experts.

Four Engines Gave Greater Range

To squelch a rumor about Fortress range on two engines versus all four, Boeing tests showed that even at light weight (40,000 lb) and sea level, the amount of power needed to keep a B-17 in the air with two powerplants shut down meant the two operating engines would work so hard that the aircraft would achieve an efficiency of 0.98 mi/gal of gasoline burned. Under the same weight and altitude conditions, Boeing found, a B-17 flying on all four engines traveled 1.4 mi/gal of gas consumed. If that weight was taken up to 5,000 ft, the four-engine economy remained about the same, but the two-engine performance dropped to about 0.95 mi/gal. Boeing tested the B-17 weighing 50,000 lb on four engines at sea level and attained mileage of about 1.25 per gallon; on two engines at this weight, the result was a dismal 0.83 mi/gal as the two engines worked ever harder to keep the Fort aloft.[36]

Rapid reverse engineering saw American-made copies of German V-1 buzz bombs slung beneath a B-17G to see if they could be carried to within 100 mi. of a target and released. The buzz bombs slowed the Fortress by about 20 mi/h. The tests did not progress to operational use. *(AAF photo.)*

The admonition to flight crews to jettison equipment when trying to get back to base with reduced power was based on solid evidence. The frigid depths of the English Channel are littered with .50-caliber machine guns, ammunition belts and boxes, and other parts and pieces of limping bombers, parts not already dropped over the Continent if fighter attack was a danger.

Notes

1. Peter M. Bowers, *Fortress in the Sky*, Sentry Books, Granada Hills, Calif., 1976.
2. *Ibid.*
3. "Employee Team Work Keeps YB-17 Project Moving on Schedule," *Boeing News*, Vol. VI, No. II, May 1936.
4. *Ibid.*
5. Peter M. Bowers, *Fortress in the Sky*, Sentry Books, Granada Hills, Calif., 1976.
6. Ray Wagner, *American Combat Planes*, Doubleday, Garden City, N.Y., 1968.
7. James R. Hansen, *Engineer in Charge—A History of the Langley Aeronautical Laboratory, 1917–1958*, National Aeronautics and Space Administration, Washington, D.C., 1987.
8. "Index of AF Serial Numbers Assigned to Aircraft 1958 and Prior—Part 1: Numerical Listing," by Procurement Division, Programmed Procurement Branch, Reports Section, MCPPSR.
9. "Windshield 'Knock-Out' Panels. BDV 288B," *Boeing Field Service News*, issue not noted.
10. "Bullet Proof Windshields. BDV 880A," *Boeing Field Service News*, Issue No. 51, 29 January 1945.
11. *Ibid.*
12. Peter M. Bowers, *Fortress in the Sky*, Sentry Books, Granada Hills, Calif., 1976.
13. Gordon Swanborough and Peter M. Bowers, *United States Military Aircraft Since 1908*, Putnam, London, 1971.
14. "Summary of the XB-40 Project," AAF documents, circa 1943, on file at the Air Force Historical Research Agency, Maxwell Air Force Base, Ala.
15. Memo, Subject: "Performance of YB-40 on Operational Mission, 29 May, 1943," from Lt. Col. William M. Reid, Commander, 92d Bomb Group, to Commanding General, VIII Air Force, 31 May 1943.
16. *Ibid.*
17. Memo, Subject: "Report on YB-40 Aircraft," from Col. William M. Reid, Commander, 92d Bomb Group, to Commanding General, Bomber Command, 7 July 1943.
18. Memo, Subject: "Performance of YB-40 on Operational Mission, 29 May, 1943," from Lt. Col. William M. Reid, 92d Bomb Group Commander, to Commanding General, VIII Air Force, 31 May 1943.
19. Indorsement to Memo, Subject: "Performance of YB-40 on Operational Mission, 29 May, 1943," from Lt. Col. William M. Reid, commander, 92d Bomb Group, to Commanding General, VIII Air Force, 31 May 1943, by Brig. Gen. H.S. Hansell, Jr., Commander, First Bombardment Wing, 1 June 1943.
20. Memo, Subject: "Report on Operation of YB-40s, 22 June, 1943," from Lt. Col. William M. Reid, Commander, 92d Bomb Group, to Commanding General, First Bombardment Wing, 23 June 1943.
21. Memo, Subject: "Report on YB-40 Aircraft," from Col. William M. Reid, Commander, 92d Bomb Group, to Commanding General, VIII Bomber Command, 7 July 1943.
22. *Ibid.*
23. *Ibid.*

24. Memo, untitled, from First Air Division commander re: request to transfer YB-40 aircraft, 12 July 1943 (in Air Force Historical Research Agency, Maxwell Air Force Base, Ala.).

25. "Summary of the XB-40 Project," AAF documents, circa 1943, on file at the Air Force Historical Research Agency, Maxwell Air Force Base, Ala.

26. Wellwood E. Beall, vice president in charge of engineering, Boeing Aircraft Co., "Design Analysis of the Boeing B-17 Flying Fortress," *Aviation Magazine,* January 1945.

27. *Ibid.*

28. *Ibid.*

29. *Ibid.*

30. *Ibid.*

31. George W. Gray, *Frontiers of Flight—The Story of NACA Research,* Alfred A. Knopf, New York, N.Y., 1948.

32. Frederick A. Johnsen, editor, *Winged Majesty—The Boeing B-17 Flying Fortress in War and Peace,* Bomber Books, Tacoma, Wash., 1980.

33. *Ibid.*

34. "Elevator Fabric Attachment Revised," *Boeing Field Service News,* Issue No. 9, 21 June 1943.

35. "Classroom in the Sky," *Boeing Field Service News,* Issue No. 4, 12 April 1943.

36. "2-Engine vs. 4-Engine Range," *Boeing Field Service News Digest,* Issues Nos. 1–25, date not noted.

Bombs Away!

The Flying Fortress Goes to War

The decision to prosecute the war against Germany with fleets of heavy bombers such as the B-17 set in motion the great irony of consuming vast quantities of Allied petroleum resources often for the purpose of destroying vast quantities of German petroleum resources. One computation figured that a single B-17 flying from England to a target at Emden, Germany, and returning to England, would carry 5000 lb of bombs and 10,000 lb of gasoline for the round trip. Less than one-third of the gasoline actually contributed to the flight of the B-17; 70 percent was wasted as 1 ton of it dissipated in cooling and 2.5 tons passed into the exhaust stream.[1] Efficient or not, the internal combustion engine would have to do. As the war progressed, telltale vapor trails from Fortress exhausts grew in number as the marvel of American production capacity overwhelmed attrition.

Sometimes strategic, sometimes tactical, sometimes pivotal, sometimes anecdotal, sometimes experimental, but nonetheless heroic, the following vignettes of the Flying Fortress's global war illuminate the B-17 and the men who understood how—and why—to use it.

Fortresses Against the Rising Sun

While peace, or its fading illusion, still embraced the United States in 1941, the AAF computed how many B-17s would be required to stand comprehensive patrols around the Hawaiian Islands to preclude the possibility of a surprise attack there. The planners deduced 72 B-17Ds would do the job. By the end of 1941, there were only 198 Fortresses of all models in the service worldwide,[2] and the AAF could ill afford to dispatch well over one-third of them to patrol paradise. Some were in stateside training use; a few belonging to the 19th Bomb Group made their way to Clark Field in the humid Philippines.

Army Air Forces B-17s entered—literally—the World War II combat arena on 7 December 1941 when a flight of unarmed 19th Bomb Group B-17s from California arrived over Oahu in the middle of the Japanese surprise attack on Hawaii. (Some photos indicate a few guns may have been carried in some positions, but the inbound Forts, low on fuel, were not

The Flying Fortress's war in the Pacific was Spartan and devoid of the niceties of England. Members of the Fifth Bomb Group posed informally with a 1-ton bomb intended for loading aboard the B-17E *Oklahoma Sooner* on Guadalcanal for release over the Japanese base at Munda. *(Thomas Hanchett collection.)*

equipped to defend themselves properly.) The B-17s landed at several airfields during the attack; one nested in a golf course when no safe runways could be found.

Beyond Hawaii

Beyond Hawaii, the AAF garrison at Clark Field in the Philippines awaited reinforcing by the B-17s that were besieged at Pearl Harbor. There simply were not enough Flying Fortresses available. Across the international dateline, it was 8 December in the Philippines as the AAF learned of the Japanese attack on Pearl Harbor. B-17s at Clark trundled out to the runway and took off around 9:30 that morning as a preventive measure when unidentified inbound aircraft were spotted over Lingayen Gulf. Two and a half hours later, with the Fortresses back on the ground at Clark and refueling, Japanese warplanes appeared overhead, executing deadly low-level strafing runs. In their wake, the attackers left about 80 men dead, and most of the Fortresses' maintenance facilities in a shambles. By 9 December, Japanese air attacks on Clark, Iba, and Nichols Fields scratched about half of the American Far East Air Forces (FEAF) from the rosters of serviceable planes. Seventeen of the 35 Fortresses in the country were all that remained in commission one day into the Philippines' fight.[3]

The following day, Capt. Colin P. Kelly, Jr., swung his 14th Bomb Squadron B-17 onto the end of the runway and roared off to join an attack on a Japanese convoy unloading troops and equipment at two locations. Captain Kelly attacked an escorting warship at Aparri. After the fact, it appears almost certain Captain Kelly and crew obtained near misses against the Japanese cruiser *Ashigara*. As the crew returned to Clark Field, their Fortress was beset by Japanese fighters that managed to bring the small-tailed early B-17 crashing to earth. In the hectic confusion of the day, at a time when Japanese forces seemed unstoppable, Colin Kelly was given credit for sinking a Japanese battleship, for which he was posthumously awarded the Distinguished Service Cross. (Pilots frequently received honors higher than those accorded the rest of their crews for wartime bomber operations in which all the men shared the danger.) This many years after the pitched battles in Philippine skies, the valor of Captain Kelly and his crew is unassailable, even if their feat may have been exaggerated in those dark and confusing days.[4]

Into early 1942, the few remaining B-17s in FEAF attacked Japanese shipping or, as on 11 January, troops moving onto the island of Tarakan. As early as 14 January 1942, with the conclusion of the U.S.–British Arcadia conference, agreement was reached to emphasize prosecution of the European war while striving to contain the Japanese. This would lead to the shaping of the bomber force arrayed against Europe, where B-17s would be emphasized, even as large numbers of B-24s filled the ranks there as well. The use of B-17s in fighting the Japanese would initially grow and then diminish until, during 1943, the last Pacific F-model was removed from combat.

Fifth Bomb Group mustered a handful of B-17Es in late 1942 or early 1943, photographed by copi-lot Joe Voellmeck on a mission, most likely to Bougainville.

While their counterparts in the Philippines continued to wage war on the Japanese invaders, a half-dozen B-17s from Hawaii, under the leadership of Lt. Col. Walter C. Sweeney, deployed to Palmyra for service with Task Group 8.9. They subsequently moved on to Canton Island, where they engaged in antisubmarine patrols before relocating to Nandi on 21 January. On 30 January, the Fortresses returned to Hawaiian soil. If they did not thwart hordes of Japanese submarines, these six B-17s helped write the book on long Pacific overwater operations and the logistics and navigational problems associated with such missions. Much attention has been directed toward the deliberate development and deployment of long-range bombers in the air war against Germany as the ultimate expres-

A B-17E of the Fifth Bomb Group, its wings festooned with search radar antennas and its upper sur-faces given variegated camouflage, flew in the vicinity of the Japanese-held target with bomb bay doors open. *(Joe Voellmeck photo.)*

Its legend, *Tokyo Termite,* barely visible, a former combat B-17E was photographed at the 13th Air Depot on New Caledonia in 1943. *(AAF.)*

sion of the Army Air Forces' vision. And yet the war in the Pacific, if fought on a smaller scale, was no less dependent on the reach of American four-engine bombers to bomb or bypass Japanese installations selectively as the American forces gained momentum, making the pioneering flights of Colonel Sweeney's Fortresses significant.

Before B-24s took over as the heavy bomber of the Pacific, B-17s flew many hectic missions in the first year of the war, such as a solo Flying Fortress photo reconnaissance sortie

The chariot of champions, B-17s were employed by many general officers as transports. This B-17E, nicknamed *Sally,* served Fifth Air Force commander Gen. George C. Kenney, a Pacific war innovator. *(Larry Jaynes collection.)*

over Wake Island on Valentine's Day 1942. On 23 February 1942, Fifth Air Force mounted its first B-17 raid on the Japanese stronghold at Rabaul. The heavies launched out of Townsville, Australia, but mechanical problems and bad weather winnowed the force down to only one B-17 bombing the target. The impending fall of Java removed more airfields from Allied use early in 1942. On 2 March, five B-17s and three export-model Liberators performed transport duty, evacuating a total of 260 men from Jogjakarta, the last available Javanese airfield. Even as the Fortresses retreated to Australia, they were not safe from attack. In the midmorning of 3 March, Broome, Australia, came under Japanese air attack; a pair of B-17s were among the casualties.[5]

Efforts to place American forces where they were most needed involved a measure of forecasting the future of the war. On 25 February 1942, Maj. Gen. Lewis H. Brereton arrived in India from the Netherlands East Indies; on 5 March, he formally took command of 10th Air Force, and its fleet of only eight Flying Fortresses, even as his Air Force's headquarters, formed in the United States, was in the process of moving overseas. Between 8 and 13 March 1942, General Brereton's handful of B-17s in India was pressed into service as transports, airlifting 29 tons of supplies and 474 troops from India to Magwe. In a textbook airlift, the Forts evacuated 423 civilians on their return sorties from Magwe. Nor were these the only evacuations performed by Fortresses engaged in the war against Japan. As the Philippine crisis worsened, on 16 March 1942, a trio of Fortresses from the embattled 19th Bomb Group began the evacuation of resident Gen. Douglas MacArthur and his family from Del Monte airfield to Australia. Ten days later, three B-17s from the 19th Group also carried Philippine President Quezon and his family to the relative safety of Australia.

By 12 April, the B-17 forces ousted from portions of the Philippines were attacking what once was the AAF's own Nichols Field there from Mindanao. On 16 April, 10th Air Force put a half-dozen B-17s aloft from Calcutta, India, bombing Rangoon in darkness with the aid of flares. The intensity of Japanese searchlights at Rangoon made bomb damage assessment impossible. The few Fortresses in India roared over the lost airfield at Myitkyina only 4 days after the Japanese succeeded in taking it. By damaging the runways and parked aircraft, the B-17s out of India sought to protect the air transport route into China from Japanese fighters that could use Myitkyina. The scarcity of assets in the war against Japan made such seemingly tactical strikes embody strategic importance.

Midway Island

As early as 18 May 1942, Seventh Air Force in Hawaii was alerted to the possibility of a Japanese attack impending against Midway Island. During this period, some crews of the Fifth Bomb Group in Hawaii still flew twin-engine Douglas B-18s, which were replaced by B-17s as quickly as possible. At this time, Fifth Air Force sent Fortresses against Rabaul, and 11th Air Force used a few B-17s to eye the Aleutians even as 10th Air Force's B-17s returned over Myitkyina and Rangoon. In the mid-Pacific, the men of the Fifth and 11th Bomb Groups readied for a showdown at Midway. On 30 May, the first B-17s began migrating from Oahu to Midway. The motley fleet of Fortresses assigned to Midway duty included newer B-17Es as well as a few of the old small-tailed D-models still on hand.[6]

On 3 June, following a sighting of Japanese ships, nine of the Midway Fortresses struck the first blow of the battle, targeting, but missing, transport elements of the Japanese fleet. Over the next three furious days of combat around Midway, B-17s tallied 55 sorties during which two Fortresses were lost, one with its crew. On 4 June, the pivotal day when U.S. Navy SBD Dauntless dive bombers sank three of four Japanese aircraft carriers in a matter of minutes, 14 B-17s also earlier attacked, but did not hit, the carrier force.[7]

Bombing from 20,000 ft to avoid the wrath of some of the Japanese fleet's gunners, the B-17s had been split off into elements of one to three bombers as a result of their search for the Japanese aircraft carriers. This diluted the bomb pattern the B-17s could achieve against any one ship. The aircraft carriers could execute hard turns to avoid the falling bombs from the bays of the Fortresses high overhead, but the Japanese paid dearly for these maneuvers as some of their returning aircraft were forced to ditch or try landing on an impossibly gyrating deck. Later that day, six B-17s en route from Hawaii bombed ships 170 mi from Midway, claiming hits on the already damaged and burning aircraft carrier *Hiryu,* a victim of SBD attacks later than the other three carriers. *Hiryu* was soon abandoned by the Japanese, and slipped beneath the Pacific Ocean the next morning.[8]

When the fires of Midway were barely out, and the sea had just glossed over the locations of the sunken aircraft carriers, on 20 June 1942, AAF headquarters published statistics showing a total of 55 B-17 sorties between 3–5 June, during which 315 bombs dropped from the Fortresses' bomb bays. The Midway B-17s typically carried 500- or 600-lb bombs, although eight 300-pounders were recorded for the 5 June action.[9]

The Dauntless dive bombers' successes at Midway had major impact on the playout of the rest of the war in the Pacific, as the heart of Japan's naval aviation might was mortally wounded there. The B-17s, though not victors over capital ships at Midway, were nonetheless crewed by earnestly brave airmen bent on contributing to the victory. Midway was joined by other air/sea engagements during the war that tended to unseat the cherished belief in the ability of heavy bombers to sink defended ships underway. If the ships under attack could throw up an antiaircraft curtain sufficient to keep the heavy bombers at altitude, the additional time for bomb travel meant the ships gained precious moments for maneuvering away from the expected paths of the explosives released by the bombers.

Bowing Out of Pacific Combat

The veteran Fifth Bomb Group was tasked to send its most experienced Fortress squadron to the South Pacific from Hawaii in mid-September 1942. The 72d Bombardment Squadron responded, along with elements of the 31st Squadron, bolstering the sister 11th Bomb Group. The Forts operated out of contested Guadalcanal. Their targets ranged from airfields, to sector patrols over the sea, to Japanese troop concentrations challenging American Marines near Henderson Field. In the October–November 1942 period, Fifth Bomb Group B-17 crews on three occasions challenged four-engine Japanese flying boats in aerial combats, for which the B-17 crews claimed two down and one damaged.[10]

By February–March 1943, the wear and tear of combat in the wilds of the vast Pacific was beginning to show on the Fifth Group's B-17s, some of which had logged more than 1000 hours. An influx of new Consolidated B-24 Liberators began replacing the Fortresses of the Fifth Bomb Group at that time as the era of the Flying Fortress in Pacific combat was drawing to a close. As late as 27 July 1943, the 31st Bomb Squadron of the Fifth Group posted six B-17s on a strike against Tarawa in the Gilbert Islands.[11] About 2 months later, the last of the Fifth Bomb Group had converted to Liberators. This matches an AAF statistical summary showing a drop in the number of B-17s arrayed in theaters of operations versus Japan from 67 first-line Fortresses in September 1943 to only three the following month and none by year's end.[12] Still, on 25 September, Fifth Air Force (not to be confused with Fifth Bomb Group, although the bomb group members said such confusion happened, sometimes to their perceived disadvantage) had B-17s in a bombing operation with B-24s and B-25s that was spread between Bogadjim and some villages on the Markham and Ramu Rivers. Even as the B-17 was being groomed for the big show over Europe, it was bowing out of Pacific combat, leaving that arena to long-ranging Convair B-24 Liberators until the advent of the first of the bigger Boeing B-29 Superfortresses in mid-1944.

Rivalries among groups of airmen are the stuff of legends. Fifth Air Force's 43d and 90th Bomb Groups were no exception; an added catalyst may have been the 1943 period when

When not muddy, the soil of Guadalcanal was readily blown around by this Fifth Air Force B-17F (41-24535) performing an engine run-up as refuelers watched. *(Joe Voellmeck photo.)*

the 43d still flew their beloved old B-17s while the 90th operated B-24 Liberators. When a 43d Group B-17 on reconnaissance clarified that a 90th Group B-24 crew had reported rocks at sea as being a Japanese convoy, the crews at the 90th sought a way to take some of the wind out of the 43d's sails. The Liberator men set out a feast, washed with quantities of Australian beer, and hosted their Fortress counterparts. Accepting the invitation, the men of the 43d Bomb Group convoyed their way to the 90th Bomb Group encampment where an outhouse had been erected and emblazoned with a sign proclaiming it to be the headquarters of the 43d Bomb Group! Fifth Air Force commanding officer Gen. George Kenney recalled that the B-17 men pretended to ignore the affront, enjoying the meal and the beer in the restful tropic evening. But early next morning, the roar of Wright Cyclone engines heralded the treetop approach of a lone 43d Group B-17. A special linking of incendiary .50-caliber ammunition was expended by a gunner aboard the B-17 as the outhouse effigy splintered and ignited under a hail of bullets. The Fortress droned on over the hills. General Kenney's subsequent admonition to both bomb groups was tempered by his understanding of the value of high-spirited competition for morale. While the general said he had not seen or heard anything, and knew nothing, he did not expect any similar event to occur again![13]

In the August 1943 issue of the *Air Forces General Information Bulletin*, during the twilight of B-17 operations against Japan, a brief account described a carefully choreographed attack by three Nakajima Hayabusa ("Oscar") fighters against a lone Fortress conducting armed reconnaissance in the southwest Pacific: "First,

On the way to Shortland Harbor, a Fifth Bomb Group B-17F (41-24457) swept past Japanese flak bursts. *(Joe Voellmeck photo.)*

A documentary drawing of a combat action involving a Pacific B-17 and three Japanese Army Naka-jima Hayabusa (Oscar) fighters was printed in the *Air Forces General Information Bulletin* in August 1943, near the end of Pacific Fortress service. The action depicted Oscars 1 and 2 closing on the Fortress from head-on, each dropping a bomb 1,500 ft above. The bombs detonated at the B-17's altitude, but the Oscar pilots slightly misjudged the range, and the bombs went off ahead and to the right of the Fortress, causing no damage. After dropping their bombs, Oscars 1 and 2 executed a full 360-degree turn and faced the Fortress again, firing from 400 yd out. The two Japanese fighters passed close under the belly of the B-17, breaking to the right and left and weaving evasively as they increased the distance between themselves and the American bomber. Meanwhile, Oscar 3 pressed an attack from the 3-o'clock level position, also passing under the Fortress to make his exit at the 8-o'clock position. Through it all, the B-17 took hits but survived the orchestrated attack to report it back at base.

Oscars No. 1 and 2, traveling head-on toward the bomber, each dropped a bomb from 1,500 feet above it. The bombs exploded at the level of the B-17 but slightly to the right and ahead, and caused no damage." The prewar concept of dropping bombs on bombers in flight seldom lived up to its premise. The two attackers next executed a 360-degree turn to their left, rolling out to face the Fortress head-on and closing from 400 yd, firing until they whipped close beneath the B-17, passing under the tail before breaking to the left and right and weaving evasively out of respect for the Fort's gunners. "Almost simultaneously," the AAF report said, "Oscar No. 3 attacked from 3 o'clock level, passed under the B-17 and broke off at 8 o'clock." Though the Fortress was punctured by its attackers, its injuries were not mortal.[14]

The withdrawal of B-17s as first-line bombers from Fifth Air Force's 43d Bomb Group by September 1943 did not mean the end of the line for all B-17s in the Pacific. Eight were spread around transport units of the 54th Troop Carrier Wing. Units operating B-17s as armed transports included the 375th Troop Carrier Group's 57th Squadron and the 433d Troop Carrier Group's 69th Squadron. As heavily gunned transports, these B-17s could make aerial deliveries where unarmed C-47s dared not fly. The American troop force landing at Los Negros in the Admiralty Island group in February 1944 received about 12 tons of guns, ammunition, plasma, and barbed wire in the first day of battle, airdropped by B-17s. To help American soldiers secure the contested airstrip at Momote, B-17F (41-24353) of the 433d Troop Carrier Group fought off fighters, airdropped ammo, and loitered to strafe Japanese positions for almost an hour. The April 1944 invasion at Hollandia, New Guinea, saw armed B-17 airdroppers intervene. By May 1944, soldiers in combat on Biak received new boots via B-17 aerial delivery.[15]

The evolution of modified B-17Gs carrying airdroppable lifeboats (sometimes these Fortresses were called B-17Hs; more often they were known as SB-17Gs) meant some of these angels of mercy for ditched aircrews would be deployed to the vast Pacific in 1945 to exotic places like Zamboanga and Ie Shima.

By the summer of 1945, eight B-17Gs carrying lifeboats joined the Fourth Emergency Rescue Squadron (ERS) at Saipan and Iwo Jima. An AAF digest of the time noted, "a B-17 with full armament and the extended range provided by Tokyo tanks can fly in and drop this self-propelled means of getaway to crews down close to enemy shores where the rescue DD [destroyer] or sub cannot navigate."[16]

The Middle East, 1942

When General Brereton was ordered to the Middle East from India in late June 1942, he brought along seven B-17Es of the 9th Bombardment Squadron of his 10th Air Force. As the new commander of United States Army, Middle East Air Forces (USAMEAF) in Cairo, General Brereton's command in 1942 was a sometimes rag-tag bunch of B-24s and B-17s convened quickly to challenge German Gen. Erwin Rommel's ability to wage war in the desert. By 2 July 1942, Brereton's B-17s were engaged in a nighttime raid on Tobruk harbor in concert with B-24s, an often repeated occurrence during this period. By the 20th of the month, nine B-17s of the Ninth Bomb Squadron and 19 Liberators of the Hal Bomb Squadron (evolved from the pioneer Halpro, or Halverson Detachment) were organized together as the First Provisional Group under the command of Col. Harry Halverson at Lydda.[17]

The number of first-line B-17 bombers in the Mediterranean Theater of Operations (MTO) hovered between 10 and 11 from July through October 1942, leaping to 64 by November of that year, coinciding with the introduction of the 97th and 301st Bomb Groups under 12th Air Force there. Tobruk continued to draw the attention of Fortress crews for much of the year. On 16 November, the relocated 97th Bomb Group, which on 17 August had flown the first U.S. heavy bomber mission out of a base in England, now waged war in Africa when a half-dozen of its Fortresses left Algiers to attack the Sidi Ahmed airfield at Bizerte.

Meanwhile, as force structure was still evolving in the MTO, Ninth Air Force still had jurisdiction over some B-17s, which were used on 18 November 1942 to bomb docks and marshaling yards at Bengasi, Libya. On the following day, P-38s escorted B-17s of 12th Air Force in a raid on the El Aouina airfield. Conditions in North Africa in November could include gooey mud at airfields. On the 28th of the month, 35 B-17s of 12th Air Force's 97th and the recently arrived 301st Bomb Group rose to attack the Bizerte dock area and airfield. The Fortresses' intended P-38 protection was thwarted by the mud. The unescorted bombers gave up two of their number to Axis fighters that day over Bizerte. These would not be the last Fortresses downed in the MTO in 1942. Two more succumbed during an escorted mission over Bizerte's harbor on the day after Christmas 1942. Transportation-related targets dominated the MTO Fortresses in 1942.[18]

England, 1942

If daylight strategic bombardment proponents were compelled to prove the merit of their claims once America entered the war, the Eighth Air Force, assigned to bases in England, was the vanguard of that effort. On 31 March 1942, Maj. Gen. Carl Spaatz suggested the Eighth Air Force, then without a specific assignment, be designated the core of the Army Air Forces in Britain (AAFIB). (By 2 May of that year, Spaatz was named commander of the Eighth AF.) On 7 April 1942, the War Department formalized the establishment of Eighth Air

Force in England, setting in motion an incredible and growing air armada that gave the B-17 its ultimate venue to elaborate on the concepts of daylight strategic bombardment. In April 1942, Lt. Gen. H.H. Arnold said: "It has become increasingly apparent that our present action in endeavoring to meet Axis threats throughout the world results in a defensive policy which cannot bring the war to a successful conclusion. To continue such a policy may well result seriously if not disastrously." General Arnold's formula for taking the war away from the Germans included attaining air supremacy by forcing the Germans to suffer higher attrition than production.[19]

The following year, the Casablanca conference produced an Allied codification of strategic target priorities that listed submarine construction facilities, aircraft industry, ball-bearing production, oil refineries, synthetic rubber plants, and vehicle production capacity. But looming over these targets was the specter of the Luftwaffe and the undiminished need to neutralize its might. Casablanca conferees said failure to blunt German fighter power could jeopardize successful Allied prosecution of the war. The Luftwaffe had to be stopped to ensure the ability to wage war against the listed strategic targets.[20]

B-17Es began arriving in the United Kingdom late in July 1942, assigned to the 97th Bomb Group. Since the 97th was in place before Eighth Fighter Command was set up to support missions with fighter escorts, Royal Air Force Spitfire Mark IX fighters were initially identified for high-altitude escort to the limits of the Spitfire's range.

Even as Flying Fortresses already were in combat in the Middle East and the Pacific, Eighth Air Force launched its inaugural B-17 mission on 17 August 1942, sending a dozen

The English tarmac was wet with rain as a 390th Bomb Group crew arrived at their B-17F to start a mission circa 1943. There appears to be a de facto distinction between officers and enlisted on this crew, with the enlisted members wearing A-2 jackets and leather flying helmets, whereas the officers had shearling coats and suitably rumpled "50-mission crush" hats. *(Jerry Cole collection.)*

B-17Es of the 97th Bomb Group against a target in western Europe for the first time. Marshaling yards at Rouen-Sotteville in France were hit by the small bomber force. RAF Spitfires provided protection, but one German fighter got within range of B-17 gunner Sgt. Kent R. West, who is credited with being the first Eighth Air Force gunner to score a fighter kill.[21]

Two days later, the Eighth's second bombing mission was part of an incursion into France by 5000 ground troops at Dieppe. Twenty-two B-17s targeted Luftwaffe airfields in an effort to occupy the German Air Force and keep it from challenging the troops at Dieppe. Extensive damage at Abbeville/Drucat was noted by the bombers. While this mission was an effective application of B-17s to reach the German-held airfields, its results were more tactical than strategic.

Repeat visits by the B-17Es to Abbeville prompted the Luftwaffe to withdraw 20 of 30 Fw-190 fighters at that field, taking them farther inland. Early B-17 missions with Spitfire escorts gave the Germans pause. Then, on 21 August, a dozen Fortresses sent to attack a target in the Low Countries were a little over a quarter-hour late making their rendezvous with the short-legged Spitfires, which by then had only enough gasoline to escort the B-17Es halfway across the English Channel. The nine remaining B-17s (three had to abort for mechanical problems) were given a recall order as they approached the coast of Holland. German fighters made the intercept and dueled with the bombers for the next 20 minutes. It was sobering for both sides, as two of the fighters fell to the B-17s' massed .50-caliber gunfire which hurled heavier rounds than British bombers typically fired at the Germans. But the Luftwaffe probed the B-17 formation, and five Fw-190s ganged up on a straggling Fortress. One German fighter pilot paid for an attack on the Fort's tail when the B-17 tail gunner shot him down. Exploding rounds from the Fw-190s' 20-mm cannons mortally wounded the lone B-17's copilot and damaged the engines on the right wing. Though this B-17 limped back to the safety of an English airstrip, its fate almost certainly would have been sealed had it been deeper inside the European continent when the combat began.[22]

The early forays by B-17Es in shallow penetrations of western Europe, often made in sunny weather that later would be remembered fondly by crews battling undercasts, tended to enhance the reputation of the Americans in a skeptical English environment. The rigors of high-altitude flight, where oxygen masks and insulated clothing were mandatory, seemed to catch the fancy of the British press. One English reporter said the American secret was the employment of robust men for the bomber aircrews, a notion that seemed to gain even more credence when a British doctor who went on a B-17 flight to observe the Americans passed out. But valuable as these early missions were for developing Fortress bombing rationale, everyone knew that tougher targets must be hit if the B-17s were to have any hope of making good on the promise of strategic bombardment advocates to demonstrably shorten the war.[23]

By 27 August, the new 92d Bomb Group's four B-17 squadrons were in place in England. On 6 September, Eighth Air Force incurred its inevitable first B-17 combat losses. The first Eighth AF Fortress to go down in the ETO in combat was over Flasselles, taking hits from three Fw-190s while on a mission to bomb the Potez aircraft plant at Meaulte, France. Observers watched four crewmen ride parachutes away from that stricken Fortress. The second B-17 loss of the mission remained a mystery: A Fortress last seen near Beachy Head and struggling to make Dover went missing. Other B-17 crews reported during debriefing that the attacking German fighters had yellow noses, a recognition symbol soon to become a fearsome sign to the stoic bomber airmen.[24]

Early German press accounts misidentified the American Fortresses as British bombers, sometimes going so far as to call them Lancasters. The Americans took this as deliberate subterfuge by Nazi propagandists who wanted to delay as long as possible acknowledging the presence of a new enemy—Americans—over the Continent. And until Fortresses began crashing down on the Continent in numbers, such a fiction was relatively easy to maintain because the altitude at which the B-17 crews worked made identification from the ground difficult.

Even as Eighth Air Force was beefing up its contingent of Fortresses in England, American and British planners were evolving war plans that would affect the deployment of the bombers. Two arguments for opening a second front against the Germans were advanced. On one hand, a second front would spread German military assets to the advantage of the beleaguered Soviets. Second, if that new front happened to be an American emphasis in North Africa, the British forces already there could gain some relief from the relentless German Afrika Korps. AAF planners were reluctant to embrace a major campaign in North Africa in the late 1942–early 1943 time frame because this threatened to dilute the numbers of heavy bombers, including B-17s, that Eighth Air Force could amass in England for coordinated attacks against German targets on the European continent.

One AAF position argued that the use of mass formations of B-17s from England constituted a second front in itself—a front defined in the skies overhead instead of on the battlefields below. In fact, a popular wartime documentary about the B-17, *Memphis Belle,* picked up this theme, calling the air war an "air front." Major General Ira Eaker argued on behalf of the validity of this assertion because concentrated B-17 missions over western Europe required the Luftwaffe to shift assets there, giving the Soviets some respite. The AAF maintained that before any invasion of the Continent could take place, the Allies had to own the skies overhead. The confrontation between Eighth Air Force and the Luftwaffe would contribute substantially to this outcome.[25]

Operation Bolero

Realistically, the Allies could not hope to mount a sustainable invasion of the Continent in 1942 because insufficient war materiel and troops were available at that time. An invasion of western Europe was contemplated for 1943, with the AAF securing mastery of the skies in the meantime. To support the ultimate invasion plans, the AAF instated Operation Bolero, the mass movement of aircraft and units to England, beginning in mid-1942. Fortresses and Liberators were among the assets earmarked for movement to England under the banner of Bolero. It was an ambitious undertaking that set the tone for thousands of B-17s and B-24s to fly the Atlantic.

The first movement overseas under Bolero saw 18 B-17s lift off from Presque Isle in northeastern Maine on 23 June 1942, bound for Goose Bay, Labrador. Three of these early B-17Es made forced landings in Greenland, and their crews were rescued. (Decades later, a Bolero B-17E nicknamed *My Gal Sal* was retrieved from where it had crash-landed in Greenland and brought to Oregon, intended for restoration.) On 1 July 1942, B-17E number 41-9085 chirped its tires on the runway at Prestwick, Scotland, to become the first American-crewed tactical aircraft to arrive in the United Kingdom by air for the war effort. As August 1942 drew to a close, 386 AAF aircraft, including 119 B-17s, had made the North Atlantic migration to England. By 1 January 1943, 882 aircraft of all types had successfully negotiated the Bolero air routes; 920 planes had attempted the crossing. One attempt that would continue to fire the imaginations of historic aircraft retrievers for years saw a B-17, acting as long-range navigational support for a half-dozen P-38s, go down on the Greenland ice along with all six of the P-38s. Inclement weather and bogus enemy radio broadcasts contributed to the forced landings of these seven Bolero participants.[26]

An August 1942 annex to the Bolero training directive detailed how B-17Fs and B-24Ds were to be loaded for the migratory flight to the United Kingdom:[27]

B-17F	
Weight empty 34,885 [lbs.]	
Gasoline—(2450 [gal.]) 14,700 [lbs.]	
Oil—132 gals. 991 [lbs.]	
[total] 50,576 [lbs.]	
Crew and Passenger[s] (10)	
1 Pilot, 1 Co-pilot, 1 Navigator, 1 Bombardier, 1 Engineer, 1 Asst. Engineer, 1 Radio Operator, 1 Asst. Radio Operator, 1 Gunner, 1 Passenger. Crew weight includes bail-out rations, parachute, and 100 lbs. of baggage per man [total] 3,000 [lbs.]	
Emergency Equipment	
2 Life Rafts 116 [lbs.]	
50 days Emergency Ration "K" 115 [lbs.]	
45 Flares 33 [lbs.]	
Bombay [sic] fuel system 500 [lbs.]	
[total] 764 [lbs.]	
Airplane Equipment	
2 Sub-machine guns w/100 rds. per gun 42 [lbs.]	
11 Guns, Cal. .50—869 [lbs.]	
1 Gun, Cal. .30—32 [lbs.]	
Ammunition, Cal. .50—200 rds. per gun 660 [lbs.]	
Ammunition, Cal. .30—200 rds. per gun 50 [lbs.]	
1 ea. Kit, navigators 79 [lbs.]	
Bomb shackles, external B-9—60 [lbs.]	
Bomb slings 26 [lbs.]	
Maintenance equipment 300 [lbs.]	
VHF, IFF radio equipment 74 [lbs.]	
[total] 2,192 [lbs.]	
Total Weight 56,532 [lbs.]	
Max. gross take-off weight 56,600 [lbs.]	
Max. gross landing weight 44,600 [lbs.]	

The Bolero loading list points out some interesting differences between the configurations of B-17Fs and their counterpart B-24Ds in the summer of 1942. Bolero-bound Liberators had a listed empty weight of 33,600 lb—more than a half-ton lighter than that cited for B-17Fs. Yet the maximum gross takeoff weight for Bolero B-24Ds was 59,000 lb, more than a ton heavier than that for the B-17Fs. The Fortresses carried less than the Liberators.[28]

Bolero provisioners included the submachine guns in part to afford crews a measure of protection in the event they made a forced landing in a hostile region. The Bolero directive also specified: "Each bomber, not accompanied by fighters, will carry 50 each 'K' Rations, made up in ten (10) packages of five (5) rations each, on the basis of one package per crew member, to be used in case of forced landing only." Additionally, each crewman was to be issued a package of bailout rations "for use only in case of forced parachute jump. This 'Bail Out' Ration package will include five each 'Bail Out' Rations, each Ration made up as follows: 1 each 'D' Ration (Chocolate bar); 2 pkg. Malted Milk—Dextrose; 1 stick Chewing Gum; 1 pkg. Boullion Powder," the directive noted. The bailout packets were to be opened by the crewmen and their components stowed in pockets. "Warning is issued that the 'D' Ration, above mentioned, is a thirst producer and should be used sparingly and as a last resort. In no case should any of the ration be consumed except in emergency," the directive said.[29]

The ferrying of, ultimately, thousands of bombers and other aircraft from the United States to Europe was a bold migration in 1942, only 15 years after Charles Lindbergh had electrified the world by crossing the Atlantic from New York to Paris solo. The crews participating in Operation Bolero were often young and inexperienced, but earnest and persevering. They faced harsh and changing weather over the North Atlantic and Greenland, and their navigators were sometimes misled by spurious German radio signals. Ultimately, the rationale for Bolero—the proposed invasion of Europe in 1943—metamorphosed into the more realistic timetable for 1944, and some Bolero assets were diverted to North Africa from England. After Bolero was moot, the aerial migration of B-17s and other warplanes to England continued throughout the war until, by 1945, rural British depots bulged with brand-new B-17Gs awaiting combat assignments.

The agency preparing the list of items to be carried on the Bolero delivery flights to England was the Air Forces Foreign Service Concentration Command. The use of the word *Concentration* in the title may have served to underscore General Arnold's desire to amass sufficient quantities of heavy bombers before sending them into combat to maximize their effect against German targets. In reality, by the end of July 1942, an American-led invasion of North Africa under the name Operation Torch was embraced by the United States, with some objections from strategic bomber advocates. The result would be a dilution of the bomber resources immediately available in England. Maj. Gen. Carl "Tooey" Spaatz wrote to General Arnold in August 1942 advising Arnold that England was the only site from which operations could be mounted to establish air supremacy over Germany. Spaatz opined, "Until such air supremacy is established there can be no successful outcome of the war."[30] Eighth Air Force would periodically lament diversion of assets to North Africa as late as the summer of 1943 when B-24 bomb groups were dispatched from England to bolster the armada for the low-level attack on oil refineries at Ploesti.

The AAF looked upon its first Eighth Air Force 100-plane heavy bomber raid of 9 October 1942 as a landmark. B-17s, for the first time out of England joined by B-24 Liberators, targeted industrial complexes primarily in Lille, France. Locomotives and steel were the priorities that day. The Fives-Lille steel plant was picked as a textbook target for high-altitude bombing; the relative nearness of Lille was an advantage for escorting fighters, and the weather held. Only 7 weeks after the first raid by a dozen Eighth Air Force bombers, the raid on Lille was a logistics marvel. Still, aborts dwindled the available bombers, and adjunct targets further diminished the force over the primary targets to 69 bombers. Some of the bombers failed to pass within bombing distance of Lille as traffic control errors were made; their bombardiers had to unceremoniously jettison their bombs over the English Channel on the ride home. If flak was light that day over France, fighter interception was determined and long-winded. One B-24 and three Fortresses succumbed.

A common problem in tracking the air war was illustrated that day over Lille. Returning bomber crews reported a total of more than 240 encounters with enemy fighters as gunners from multiple B-17s and B-24s tracked the same enemy planes as they whipped through the American bomber formations. Inexperienced gunners initially were given credit for downing 48 Luftwaffe fighters, probably downing 38 more, and damaging another 19. Interrogators came to realize the muzzle flames spouting from the German fighters sometimes were mistaken by eager B-17 gunners as evidence of hits made on the German fighters. Later, as intelligence officers worked to eliminate duplicate and honestly erroneous claims, the tally was reduced to 21 kills, 21 probables, and 15 damaged.[31] Even this count seems optimistic by latter-day yardsticks. Perhaps it is explained by the novice way the Luftwaffe pressed home tail attacks that day, affording tail gunners ample opportunities to fire back with minimal deflection, lacing .50-caliber slugs into the fighters behind them with relative ease. One thing was certain: The Luftwaffe pilots were brave and tenacious. Fortress gunners could ill afford to relax.

Stopping Submarines Where They Live

In 1942, the AAF labored to refine and attack a series of strategic targets intended to cripple Germany's ability to wage war. The daylight precision bombing effort was a brave new world with untried schemes that could have momentous consequences. The first year of American participation in the war saw German submarines play havoc with convoys in the Atlantic, and the U-boats also were known to emit spurious radio signals in an effort to confuse the navigators of Europe-bound warplanes from the United States. If left unchecked, the U-boat fleets threatened the lifeline of supplies needed to fight the European war. In specific, the planned invasion of North Africa, Operation Torch, was threatened by the severity of the German submarine threat in the Atlantic. Army Air Forces responses included delegating long-ranging B-24D Liberators for antisubmarine patrols and sending B-17s directly over the submarines' pens on the coast of occupied France. Anglo-American discussions about how to deal with the German submarine threat included frank and seemingly simple assessments: The British lacked the ability to conduct precision bombing of the sub pens in daylight, and nocturnal area bombing would not take out these priority targets. So while the RAF assigned night bombers to attack German submarine-manufacturing facilities, the hardened sub pens were taken on by the young Eighth Air Force, perhaps innocent of what lay ahead. There was a geographic logic to it: While the AAF pondered its future escort fighter capabilities, shallow penetrations of enemy airspace to reach the sub pens seemed an appropriate use of American airpower then in England.[32]

Fifteen Fortresses executed Eighth Air Force's first attack on German submarine pens at Lorient-Keroman on 21 October 1942, when the plucky men of the 97th Bomb Group pressed an attack after cloud cover prompted some four dozen other B-17s, survivors of an inbound air battle, to abort. Three Forts had already fallen to an attack by three dozen FW-190s. Breaking with normal doctrine, the B-17s attacked from only 17,500 ft, perhaps a mile and a half lower than many operations. The 15 B-17s released a total of 30 one-ton bombs. Perhaps due to the lower altitude of release, the accuracy was high, with several of the 2000-lb bombs knocking directly into the reinforced concrete roof protecting the submarine pens. The concrete held.[33]

On the last day of that month, General Spaatz told Hap Arnold the cost of targeting the submarine pens could outweigh benefits derived. General Spaatz contemplated attacks as low as 4000 ft to improve aim and acknowledged the likelihood of higher casualties.[34]

A 7 November two-part attack on submarine pens at Brest involved 23 B-17s followed about 4 hours later by 11 B-24s from the 93d Group. The results again were disappointing; accuracy still could not breach the thick concrete of the pens. Two days later, Eighth Air Force launched a dozen Liberators at 17,500 to 18,300 ft over the submarine base at St. Nazaire, while sending 31 B-17s there at altitudes between only 7500 and 10,000 ft. The B-24s sustained but little flak damage, while the low-flying Fortresses lost three of their number outright, with 22 other B-17s in the raid coming home with antiaircraft shrapnel damage. This ended the experiment of taking Eighth AF heavy bombers down low over well-defended targets.

Yet another raid on the submarine facilities at St. Nazaire was logged on 14 November as 15 B-17s and nine B-24s made the trip. The bombers were back over the pens of St. Nazaire on 17 November; the next day, they targeted three submarine facilities at La Pallice, Lorient-Keroman, and St. Nazaire. Then, on 23 November 1942, 36 heavies over St. Nazaire provided the combat test for a new Luftwaffe tactic: frontal attacks. Traditional wisdom said bombers were best attacked from behind, but the B-17's designers were aware of this, and beginning with the E-model, Fortresses were factory-equipped with a viable tail stinger of two heavy .50-caliber machine guns. The aerial defenders of St. Nazaire decided the risks of high closing speeds in head-on attacks were worth the possibility of placing bullets into a B-17 vital spot and possibly spooking a formation into losing its tight protective cohesion. When bad weather reduced the ranks of remaining 91st and 306th Bomb Group B-17s to a total of nine B-17s between them over St. Nazaire that day, those few Fortresses took the brunt of head-on attacks. Two from the 91st dropped into death plunges and others were damaged; a Fortress from the 303d Bomb Group also was downed; only the 305th Bomb Group remained intact in what was its baptism of fire. If the startling Luftwaffe tactics were successful that day, the small size of the B-17 formations may have inadvertently helped the enemy further.

Subsequent AAF responses included a variety of beefed-up nose gun arrangements running the gamut from hand-held mounts to the ultimate power chin turret of the B-17G. Out of this need came a reinforced mount for a single forward-firing flexible .50-caliber gun that was inserted in the modified nose glazing of B-17Fs, first at the 306th Bomb Group and then by Eighth Air Service Command. The 306th's staff sergeants Ben Marcilonis and James Green thus gave many European B-17Fs a unique look and a frontal defense position that was viable until the later advent of the powered chin turret. Formations also were improved and tightened in a never-ending quest to lock the Luftwaffe out.[35]

Meanwhile, even as the Eighth Air Force studied its apparent lack of success in inflicting long-term damage to submarine pens in the wake of the fifth attack on St. Nazaire in 2 weeks, a British opinion praised the American efforts for the short-term effects they had on disrupting German submarine servicing schedules. Still, it had to be a disappointment to the architects of daylight strategic bombardment to witness their submarine pen attacks fail to demolish the concrete structures, with only a polite acknowledgment of disrupting German schedules at their bases in western France to show for the harrowing raids. By the first week of December 1942, a study by Eighth Bomber Command announced that available American bombs could not be expected to penetrate German submarine pen roofs from any altitude at which accuracy could be maintained. And still, repeat strikes like the 30 December 1942 attack on the submarine base at Lorient were beginning to show cumulative effects.[36]

Of more than 50 Fortresses in a combined B-17/B-24 attack on St. Nazaire's U-boat pens on 3 January 1943, seven B-17s were lost to fighters and flak. With 15 B-24s also on the raid, this effort was Eighth Air Force's largest attack to date on submarine facilities. New ideas were tried that day, including formation bombing with crews dropping on the work of select bombardiers. The predictability of the bombers' run against the pens may have contributed to a German defense twist that day, as flak gunners set up a predetermined barrage for the bombers to fly into rather than tracking the movement of the airplanes. That early in the war, the loss of seven B-17s representing 70 men was sobering.

B-17 and B-24 attacks on German submarine pens and the apparently less well-fortified submarine-construction facilities continued well into 1943. But this was not the air war the strategic bombardment proponents had envisioned; it was an ugly necessity prompted by the startling efficacy of German submarines in the Atlantic. As 1943 grew older on the calendar, inroads were made by Liberators ranging far out to sea, providing a more secure umbrella for Allied convoys and sinking or discouraging increasing numbers of U-boats. By

Looking back over the tail of a 390th Bomb Group B-17F, contrail fingers pointed to other B-17s and to single-engine P-47 escort fighters high overhead. Escort fighter tactics changed from closely guarding the bombers to ranging ahead to disrupt German fighter flights. *(Jerry Cole collection.)*

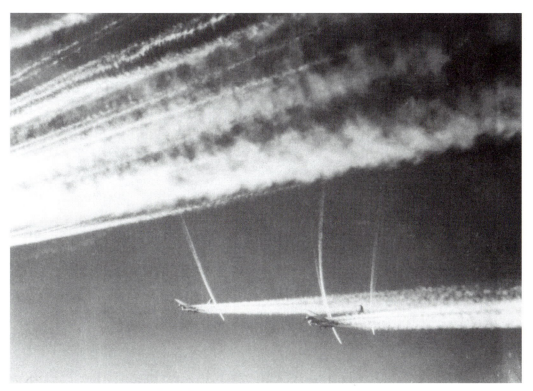

A stark counterpoint to the B-17s' unwavering contrails, escort fighters cut across at 90 degrees to protect the 390th Bomb Group bombers on a mission over Europe circa 1943. *(Jerry Cole collection.)*

The beauty of massed contrails could quickly become a mortal liability as the white streamers of condensation pointed unerringly back to the bombers that made them, highlighting them to German fighters and gunners. *(Jerry Cole collection.)*

Combat over Europe painted fantastic patterns as fighters and bombers attained altitudes where contrails could form. *(390th Bomb Group via Jerry Cole.)*

18 May, the combined Chiefs of Staff approved a combined bomber offensive (CBO) that would schedule round-the-clock attacks on the Axis by American and British aircraft. While still rating submarine yards higher than the enemy aircraft industry, ball-bearing production, or petroleum, the CBO said the destruction of Luftwaffe fighters was the first priority objective.[37]

Submarine bases and plants continued to attract Eighth Air Force attention, but the threat to convoys began to wane even as more and more B-17s became available to emphasize other target systems. Greater successes were achieved against submarines on the high seas than when the U-boats were replenished beneath concrete sanctuaries in the relative safety of occupied France.

The hardened French U-boat pens were defeated by overrunning, not by bombing. The last U-boat motored outbound from St. Nazaire on 23 September 1944. After that time, the remaining German submarines were forced to withdraw to unprotected harbors where they more readily fell prey to bombing.[38]

Bombing Through Overcast

The weather of northern Europe includes ample overcast days. In fact, in the 1970s, when the U.S. Air Force needed to replicate conditions in Germany to test A-10 camouflage schemes, they used Fort Lewis in Washington State, an area known for its rainy, gray inclement weather. In March 1945, Eighth Air Force's weather section calculated that only 73 days per year were acceptable for visually bombing targets in Germany. But strategic bombardment proponents knew about limiting weather factors over Europe long before the 1945 survey. It was strategic—and political—death for Eighth Air Force to appear idle as much as four-fifths of the year because of inclement target weather. And for the crews, repeated mission delays due to weather had telling effects on morale. At the Casablanca conference in 1943, Gen. Ira Eaker announced Eighth Air Force was sharpening the ability to bomb through overcast with British radio/radar homing devices called Oboe and Gee.

Oboe's radar used two ground stations. A controller on the ground made note of the range of both beacons from the bomber in flight, using the lapse of time between transmission of ground signals and the return of plane signals to devise a path and ranging information for the bomber to lead the aircraft to a predetermined point on the map, as depicted by the intersection of concentric signals radiating out from the two ground stations. Gee was a radio-navigation device that used three ground stations and fixed the aircraft's position by intersecting lines representing two signals. Limitations with these systems were their reliance on ground stations and a maximum range of about 200 mi for an aircraft flying at 20,000 ft. Nonetheless, in 1943, this was promising science.[39]

In use, Gee and Oboe disappointed. Gee could be jammed by the Germans, as Eighth Air Force learned during bombing missions conducted with the device in January and February 1943. And Gee's accuracy for hitting targets through overcast was not good enough, although the device was widely embraced purely for navigational purposes. Eighth Air Force next turned to Oboe as a possible solution to blind bombing, but the British only made four sets available by late March 1943, allowing two B-17s and two B-24s to be Oboe-equipped. The British were hesitant to commit many Oboe sets to the Eighth Air Force in 1943, partly because they were hand-built units in demand by the RAF and partly because the British did not want to risk Oboe over the Continent in relatively slow day bombers. It was believed nocturnal high-speed Mosquito bombers could use Oboe with a better chance of returning to the United Kingdom safely. What remained was another British advancement: H2S radar. Eighth Bomber Command believed a number of H2S-equipped heavies sprinkled strategically among a formation could increase the number of operational bombing days by 50 percent.[40]

The crew was still examining their freshly bellied B-17F as ground crewmen approached the 390th BG Fort, probably nicknamed *Spot Remover. (Jerry Cole.)*

An early 92d Bomb Group Pathfinder, Vega B-17F 42-5793 with elongated chin H2S radome fairing, was photographed over an English undercast on a practice sortie on 25 August 1943. Pathfinders dramatically increased Eighth Air Force's ability to carry the war to Germany in all kinds of weather, although limitations to the radar typically precluded their use over occupied countries, to restrict any collateral damage to Germany. *(AAF.)*

A 6 September 1943 mission to Stuttgart was largely frustrated by weather, but that made it no less deadly for 262 heavy bombers that attacked targets of opportunity in Germany and France instead. Crew milling beside a 390th Bomb Group B-17F was far more fortunate than the men aboard 45 heavies that did not return to England that day. Insignia of this Fortress carried short-lived red border. *(Jerry Cole.)*

By the spring of 1943, a B-17 in England had been fitted with H2S radar for evaluation. But the slow pace of British production and high-volume need by the RAF meant that few H2S sets were forthcoming for the Eighth Air Force. The need was to be up and running with H2S by September 1943, in time for the onset of bad weather over Europe. On 15 July 1943, the 482d Bomb Group was activated and designated a pathfinder force. It would provide radar-equipped bombers to be placed in Eighth Air Force formations. As Eighth Air Force scrambled to prepare for inclement weather, a mix of British and American H2S equivalent sets was envisioned, along with some Americanized equivalents of Oboe, called SCR-297. Ultimately, SCR-297 was abandoned as H2S and H2X came on strong.[41]

H2S, H2X, and the later Eagle radar, which was housed in a stub airfoil beneath the bomber's fuselage, all sent a beam of energy that scanned the ground and mapped it on a cathode ray tube. According to an Air Force synopsis of World War II radar development: "Navigation was possible by a comparison of the radar picture with a map. Bombing could be done by selecting the appropriate target signal, by directing the plane over it, and by feeding aircraft altitude and groundspeed to the computer which would then provide a bombing circle on the scope; coincidence of target signal and this circle indicates the proper bomb release instant."[42]

In the face of contrary weather, Eighth Air Force mustered about 18 H2S-equipped heavy bombers by December 1943; of these, about 10 were B-17s. Meanwhile, in the United States, 20 similar H2X sets were being hurried into production. H2X promised a higher degree of target resolution vital to bombing mass centers such as Berlin with any hope of accuracy. H2X also reached out with a range of about 90 mi—three times greater than Mark II H2S. To correct for any erroneous scans due to rolling motion of the bomber, H2X incorporated azimuth stabilization. A dozen B-17s received H2X sets during the summer and early fall of 1943. At Grenier Field, New Hampshire, the new radars were undergoing test operations in the Fortresses, even as crews were learning how to use the equipment. By early October, the dozen H2X-equipped Fortresses arrived in Alconbury to join their H2S counterparts in England. The first Eighth Air Force H2S mission was flown on 27 September, and the first H2X combat mission came in early November 1943.

The Eighth Air Force's inaugural H2S radar formation bombing mission in September used the German port city of Emden as a target for several reasons. Located on the coast, the terrain of Emden would clearly register on the radar scopes as a distinguishing light and dark pattern between earth and sea. Emden was less than a mile in diameter, providing a target size deemed appropriate for a test of H2S and its new operators. Attacks on Rotterdam and Hamburg had led to an increased German use of Emden, plus the dreaded German submarines were assembled there. With 9/10 cloud cover, a force in excess of 150 B-17s, representing three combat wings, observed British marker flares dropped by the Pathfinders as well as the Pathfinders' own bomb loads. The first combat wing released bombs simultaneously with the Pathfinders. As the flares wafted down over Emden with a sink rate of 500 ft per minute, the second combat wing of B-17s dropped their bombs on the markers provided by the glowing flares. By the time the third bomb wing passed over the target area, the flares had descended into the undercast, so these Fortresses selected adjacent targets of opportunity for visual bombing through breaks in the clouds. A second force of B-17s arrived over Emden, but only the first of its three wings was able to bomb with the Pathfinder's release. The second and third forces made visual bomb runs through breaks in the clouds. H2S-led heavies returned over Emden on 2 October. Reconnaissance was unavailable until the cloud cover cleared after the second raid, at which time it appeared that three bomb concentrations were achieved: in the Emden dock area, on the edge of town, and about 3 mi away beside a lake, which on radar must have resembled the harbor to the neophyte radar operators.[43]

The solid undercast suggests that these 390th Bomb Group B-17s were following a Pathfinder over Germany. *(Jerry Cole collection.)*

The debut of H2X on 3 November 1943 also marked the first time Eighth Air Force sent 500 bombers on a mission: A mixed force of 539 B-17s and B-24s, aided by nine H2X Pathfinders and two H2S-equipped aircraft, attacked the port of Wilhelmshaven. The aiming point was destroyed under the rain of bombs. The mission was escorted by P-38s which gained their first real taste of European Theater combat, during which the fighters claimed three German planes shot down.[44]

A wartime tally of Eighth Air Force missions showed 25 H2X and/or H2S missions were flown by B-17s and B-24s in 1943, starting with a single-ship attack on Frankfurt on 17 August, followed by the September Emden effort, and on through a list of German targets that culminated with a mighty 656-bomber effort over Ludwigshafen on 30 December. The bombers (not delineated by type) dropped a total of 11,601.4 tons of bombs during these sorties. No radar missions were mounted by the Eighth between 2 October and 3 November while technicians worked on problems in the radar sets that were chiefly related to pressure problems in the wave-guide systems at high altitudes. Even as problems plagued the new radars, the tonnage dropped on radar missions exceeded the tonnage released on visual missions by Eighth Air Force in the same time period. A 13 December raid over Kiel produced serious damage. General Eaker reported:

> Here is the most interesting thing about the Kiel raid. It was almost an ideal day for overcast bombing. The tops of the clouds were at about 4,000 [ft]; the markers could be clearly seen by all the combat wings; a good part of North Germany was fogged in or under very low cloud. We had pretty good reason to believe from German radio chatter that they tried to get their single engine fighters up but were unable to make it, probably losing a considerable number operationally. Some of the twin engine fighters came through but only a very small percentage of

what we are accustomed to. Our crews never saw any ground or water within 100 miles of the target. To have bombs come raining down on the city under these conditions must indeed have been a dismal prospect.[45]

General Eaker went on to extol the virtues of bombing through overcast, reiterating how discouraging it must be to the Germans, while adding: "On our side we escape two things which we suffered from last winter. The first was the discouragement to crews occasioned by continued inactivity and the second was the drop in the experience-level due to failure to fly and fight and shoot with regularity. These are very big operational factors which . . . should never be discounted."[46]

The early bombing through overcast (BTO) missions included samples of H2S, H2X, and Oboe Mark I and Mark II. From this experience, a clear preference for H2X was made by Eighth Air Force, and General Eaker urgently requested more H2X sets from General Arnold. But not all American military planners were as pleased with the 1943 BTO missions as was General Eaker. The radar sorties tended to be on coastal German cities, where terrain features were most easily discerned on the radar scopes. These targets largely excluded the German aircraft industry, considered vital to obtaining mastery of the air. General Eaker argued that the coastal targets allowed his crews to work on their radar technique, while permitting available Eighth Air Force fighters to provide escort as they honed the facets of cooperation between the fighters and bombers. General Eaker said no one was more irritated than he over the inability to demolish German fighter factories during that time period. "The fact simply is that there has been no day since November 1 when we could see the fighter factories in order to attack them visually. Instead of sitting on our hands waiting for that happy day, we have been working day and night at maximum effort on . . . the perfection of the technique and technical development of overcast bombing."[47]

Four enclosed-waist B-17Gs of the 452d Bomb Group held formation over Bordeaux, France, at 20,000 ft, no contrails to betray them. *(AAF.)*

In an eerie reflected light from the undercast, 390th Bomb Group B-17Fs with a few G-models dropped bombs, probably on cue from a radar-equipped Pathfinder aircraft over Germany. *(Jerry Cole.)*

As Eighth Air Force clamored for additional radar-equipped bombers, production H2X sets (designated AN/APS-15) arrived in England beginning in February 1944. This allowed more bomb groups to own their Pathfinders, making the logistics of mounting missions easier than relying on Pathfinders from a central pool. By January 1944, the deliberate bombing campaign against German aircraft production capacity included increased use of Pathfinders. Training aids were devised to sharpen the skills of Pathfinder navigators and bombardiers, and the 482d Bomb Group took on the seemingly incongruous role of a training unit overseas to increase the number of crews and fight the attrition that accompanied increased operations in 1944. Years later, the Cold War Strategic Air Command would use elaborate radar bomb scoring sites to verify the accuracy of its bomber crews in simulated attacks on American towns. In England in late 1944, a little ingenuity had converted an SCR-584 antiaircraft fire control radar set to function as a BTO accuracy gauge. According to an Air Force report, the SCR-584

> was used to track the plane on its practice bombing mission. From information presented on the SCR-584, the position of the plane can be plotted on a map; and, by communication channels, the imaginary release of bombs on the target can be recorded on this map. Knowing the type of bomb, plane heading, altitude and speed, and wind speed and direction, the controller can determine the point of impact and thus evaluate the student's ability.[48]

Sophisticated tools like radar demanded sophisticated thinking and training aids.

To help H2X crews refine their ability to hit precise targets, Eighth Air Force produced a series of radar maps which were photographs of the H2X display screen depicting actual targets from several approaches. Added to the target photos were radar mosaic maps of en route territory in Holland and western Germany, from which navigators could correlate elapsed flight time to features on the mosaic as compared to the scope itself. In May 1944, simplified maps were drawn that approximated what the scope would pick up and deleted the normal clutter of things on maps that only made the H2X navigator's chores harder. By July 1944, Pathfinder bombers were able to carry a camera to directly photograph their own radar scope during the mission, further adding to the log of information available for future strikes, as well as for strike analysis.

The vast majority of BTO missions were directed against Germany proper. (A significant exception to this came with H2X missions in support of the Normandy invasion in June 1944.) As General Eaker had described it, one anticipated effect of BTO was to demoralize the Germans by taking away any sanctuary the weather might have offered. Though not stated, it is also possible that Allied planners were chary of using the developmental radar bombing on targets in occupied countries, lest errors cause bombs to fall in civilian areas. As ever more H2X-equipped B-17s and B-24s became available, Eighth Air Force could launch more BTO missions. But the use of BTO techniques was still considered secondary to visual bombing, and when weather permitted, visual bombing procedures still prevailed. Bad weather coincided with increases in H2X missions; October 1944, February 1945, and March 1945 were high points in the use of H2X by Eighth Air Force. In those 3 months, H2X was employed in dropping more than 77,000 tons of bombs in about 30,000 sorties.

From January 1944 through April 1945, H2X was used for more than 51 percent of all Eighth Air Force bombing sorties against Germany, meaning that targets in Germany were hit more than twice as often as they might have been had radar bombing not been available.[49]

When visibility conditions were not decisive enough to dictate either visual or radar bombing solely, some missions employed Pathfinders to perform "synchronous bombing through overcast." According to the AAF *Bombardiers' Information File,* this coordinated the radar and the bombsight. Synchronous BTO "is usually done on night missions or on day missions when visibility is poor. Experience has shown that visual bombing missions improve when they are led by an airplane which employs this BTO combination. With the advance information he receives from the radar operator, the bombardier is less likely to make any large errors."[50]

On 28 March 1944, *Mon Tete Rouge II,* a G-model from the 452d Bomb Group, was photographed at 17,900 ft on the way to France. (*AAF photo by SSgt. Chelso V. Puiratto.*)

Wryly nicknamed "Too Little Too Late," this Eagle-equipped radar Fortress did not see actual combat in Europe. Eagle radar stub wing antenna may be seen hanging beneath the fuselage just ahead of the main landing gear. *(Gordon S. Williams collection.)*

The relationship between the bombsight and the radar scope changed depending on visibility at the target area. "When visibility is zero," the AAF Bombardiers' Information File explained, "the bombardier depends entirely upon the information he obtains from the radar operator to solve the bombing problem. As visibility improves, the bombardier takes over more of the sighting operation. In clear weather, bombing is done essentially by the bombsight, though with the effective aid of the radar equipment." The bombardier and radar operator worked together to synchronize the bombsight and radar images for accuracy. Even under visual conditions, if a radar operator was following through, he could toggle the bombs in the event of a last-minute bombsight malfunction, thereby saving the bomb run. Using information like drift angle, provided by the radar operator, the bombardier could take over the operation when visibility allowed.

In the United States, the Radiation Laboratory devised a self-contained target radar with sharp resolution, under the designation AN/APQ-7. Called *Eagle*, this unit's 16-ft antenna was housed in an 18-ft airfoil mounted beneath the fuselage of a bomber. Its acuity derived from its 0.4-degree beam width. The Eagle computer was capable of determining the slant range for bomb release in accordance with bomb type, aircraft altitude, groundspeed, and wind velocity. The Eagle computer was said to be operationally simpler and more accurate than that associated with H2X. According to a 1946 report on Eagle: "During the bomb run, a rotatable electronic cursor is placed on the target and the plane is headed so that the target tracks down the cursor toward the bomb release line; coincidence of target signal and release line indicates the instant for bomb release." Though research into Eagle began before H2X, complexities with the antenna and the urgent need for H2X (which could be made operational sooner) pushed Eagle into the background.

The first Eagle-equipped bomber was a B-17 that arrived at Alconbury on 3 October 1944, accompanied by Dr. J. H. Buck of the Radiation Laboratory. Testing and training with Eagle began immediately, involving the pioneering 482d Bomb Group. Twenty-two Eagle-

The 305th Bomb Group's triangle-G tail marking is evident on the nearest trio of B-17Fs attacking the German-held airfield at Villacoublay near Paris in August 1943. Thunderbolts provided escort into France. *(AAF.)*

equipped aircraft arrived at Alconbury during March and April 1945. (Eagle was also mounted on B-24s and, in the Pacific, B-29s.) Some operators were up to speed on the system while others were in training. Six Eagle bombers, with radar instructors as operators, were made available for combat sorties, but the rapid end of the war precluded a true combat trial over Europe. However, 21 Eagle nocturnal reconnaissance sorties were made using only Eagle for navigation. Some of these flights ranged beyond Berlin. In tests conducted by Eighth Air Force, Eagle produced a median circular error of 1100 yd, which was about half the size of the error made with H2X in similar tests. But the promise of using Eagle aboard B-17s expired with the end of the war in Europe in May 1945.

Western Europe, 1943

Evolution of the daylight precision bombing mission over Europe was hobbled by the imposition of urgent Allied airpower needs and initially compounded by the lack of sufficient numbers of bombers and escort fighters to conduct full-scale strategic aerial warfare against Germany. By May 1943, the Combined Bombing Offensive (CBO) plan devised by the United States and Great Britain did much to codify round-the-clock bombing, while elevating the urgency of neutralizing German fighter strength, since that was key to air superiority. The growing Eighth AF was able to put up 182 olive drab B-17s on 22 June 1943 to initiate the first large-scale daylight raid on the Ruhr, when a synthetic rubber plant and chemical works at Huls were targeted.[53] In the math of the era, with gravity bombs falling several miles to earth, accuracy that day was good; nearly a fourth of the bombs dropped landed right in the factory environs, stemming 30 percent of Germany's synthetic rubber production for a month and causing output to be diminished for the next half year.

On 1 July 1943, Maj. Gen. Barney Giles wrote General Arnold, emphasizing the need to increase the number of escort fighters available to protect strategic bombers. At that time, the ratio was actually less than one fighter group per four bomb groups, and General Giles said the ratio needed to be closer to one to two. The message corroborated the CBO decision

A grinning firefighter ensured that B-17 42-31092, an early Seattle G-model, of the 447th Bomb Group did not catch fire following a prop-bending belly landing back in England. *(Bob Sturges collection.)*

Jacks could help levitate a bellied-in B-17G of the 447th Bomb Group in England. Since all three blades of each propeller were bent, the engines were running at the time of impact. Low-wing Fortresses could survive belly landings better than their high-wing B-24 counterparts. *(Bob Sturges collection.)*

Even when passing on congratulations to 569th Bomb Squadron commander Col. Tuttle (left), the warrior Curtis LeMay (right) was photographed without breaking a smile.

A Fortress with a severed tail over Europe might porpoise crazily for a while, but its onrushing meeting with the earth was inevitable. *(AAF.)*

to go after German fighter strength. Two days later, General Devers wrote General Arnold that a dire need existed for high-altitude bomber gunnery training. The strategic bomber was far from the unstoppable weapon prewar planners had envisioned. Even strategic bombardment stalwarts agreed that their ability to take the war to Germany in a meaningful way could only be accomplished when German fighters were neutralized. (In the late 1990s, chief U.S. Air Force historian Richard P. Hallion would make the point that air superiority was the lowest form of security the Air Force should be willing to accept; air dominance should be the real goal. In 1943, the availability of escort fighters who could at least blunt the thrusts of the Luftwaffe would be most welcome. Air superiority was still a goal, and a level of security approaching air dominance would have to wait until the very end of the war.)

By 22 July, the British Joint Intelligence Committee said the Combined Bombing Offensive was bearing fruit already. In addition to measurable disruption of several key warmaking industries in the Ruhr, the CBO had caused the Luftwaffe to go increasingly on the defensive, arraying more than half of its fighters on the western front, at the expense of Luftwaffe fighter strength in the Mediterranean and eastern fronts. This must have been received with mixed emotions at Eighth Air Force B-17 bases in England; the success of the bombers had the effect of calling in more German fighters than before!

The deepest penetration of Germany to date, made possible in part by drop-tank-equipped P-47 Thunderbolt fighter escorts, took place on 28 July when 28 Fortresses reached the FW-190 plant at Oschersleben as 49 more targeted the aircraft works at Kassel. Good bombing results were tempered with the loss of 22 bombers; returning crews noted the Luftwaffe was getting deadly in the use of air-to-air rockets. The rockets carried an 80-lb warhead that was timed to explode. The trick was to launch the rockets at an appropri-

After the mission, Eighth Air Force debriefers like these men of the 385th Bomb Group gathered as much intelligence as they could from returning crews. Often, the truth about fighter claims and bombing results was ascertained after comparing the observations of more than one crew. *(Brown/USAFA.)*

The 390th Bomb Group photo section analyzed B-17 strike photos after missions. *(Jerry Cole collection.)*

A 96th Bomb Group B-17F received maintenance and bombs in North Africa following a telling strike on Regensberg on 17 August 1943. Curtis LeMay led the force of B-17s on an 11-hour flight from England to the target and then southwest to Africa, evidently confounding much of the German antiaircraft and fighter network in the process. *(Brown/USAFA.)*

A jagged hole let daylight through the vertical fin of 388th Bomb Group Fortress number 42-30800, a late Seattle F-model, photographed in England on 10 October 1943. (Brown/USAFA.)

ate distance (about 3000 ft) from the bombers in order to achieve detonation in proximity to the B-17s.

The Eighth Air Force observed the first anniversary of its inaugural heavy bomber operations in England by sending a force of 315 B-17s against two targets in Germany—Schweinfurt and Regensburg—on 17 August 1943, marking the new, deepest penetration to date. Though the war was far from decided and Allied air superiority was still but a goal, the presence of so many B-17s over Germany could only confirm the incredible production capacity of the United States. The emblematic confidence of the Americans presented a challenge that Germans would not shrink from, however.

The bearing manufacturing capacity at Schweinfurt and the large Messerschmitt facility at Regensburg both figured in the replenishment of the Luftwaffe. Their neutralization would help win the skies for the Allies. The Forts released 1,448,000 lb of bombs on the two targets that day, scoring telling hits. The bearing industry was able in part to relocate. The Fourth Bomb Wing force, led by the innovative and brusque Brig. Gen. Curtis LeMay, was delegated to bomb Regensburg. LeMay's brand of pragmatism sometimes caused him to swap altitude for accuracy; this day, the Regensburg force was set to bomb at altitudes between only 17,000 and 19,000 ft. These bombers suffered the deadly torment of 90 minutes of fighter attacks inbound. Seventeen Fortresses were downed in the running fight to Regensburg. On the egress, the Regensburg attackers threw the Luftwaffe a curve and headed south toward an eventual landing in North Africa 11 hours after takeoff. Exit attacks

Though sheet-metal mechanics wrought wonders in England, even some Flying Fortresses were deemed too far gone to resuscitate. Then they became fair game for resourceful scavengers who unbolted and cut parts and pieces off to repair less severely damaged B-17s. (Jerry Cole.)

Armorers used handles resembling hay hooks to grab the front lug of 100-lb bombs for loading aboard a 388th Bomb Group B-17 in England on 24 August 1943. *(Brown/USAFA.)*

A hoist jacked a 2000-lb bomb up into the bay of a 385th Bomb Group B-17 in England on 21 September 1943. *(Brown/USAFA.)*

This 390th BG crew was happy to put caricatures of Axis leaders behind the eight ball to signify their plight according to American pool-hall slang. *(Jerry Cole.)*

were lighter. In the pocked and smoking ruins of Regensburg lay mangled jigs for the fuselage of a new secret fighter—the jet-powered Me-262—although General LeMay and his men could not have known of this good fortune.

The other portion of the day's strategic bombardment menu was a force of B-17s of the First Bomb Wing sent to Schweinfurt. The Luftwaffe responded with the weight of its western European single-engine forces, pitting an estimated 200 fighters against the 230 First Wing B-17s. Thirty-six of these Fortresses did not return to England. All told, 60 B-17s did not survive Schweinfurt and Regensburg that summer day.[54]

In the heat of battle—one of the bloodiest single engagements over Europe—B-17 gunners at first claimed a total of 288 German fighters shot down that day, later scaled back to 148. The real figure may have been as low as only 25 fighters destroyed in the air. If the claims were at first high, the relentless nature of the attacks caused many gunners to open fire. How could accurate accounting prevail in a sky filled with bucking bombers, headlong racing fighters, and thousands of spinning bullets? Perhaps it was fortuitous that cloudy weather following the anniversary raids forestalled any efforts to return deep over Germany. As AAF planners would acknowledge again later in the year, such losses were not sustainable on a recurring basis.

On 25 August, Eighth Air Force heavy bombers began participation in Operation Starkey. These attacks in the west were intended to engage the Luftwaffe and keep those German assets from migrating back to the east, while rehearsing attacks for the impending invasion of the Continent. The desire to draw the Luftwaffe up to fight was largely frustrated, and the operation failed to make serious inroads into German fighter strength.

Stuttgart, Germany, hosted other bearing and aircraft industries and was the target of 338 of a record 407 heavy bombers dispatched by Eighth Air Force on 6 September. The other 69 heavies were B-24s that deliberately flew a diversion over the North Sea. Thickening undercast on the Continent foretold of an obscured target, but the B-17s droned on. Near Stuttgart, Luftwaffe fighters were unleashed to perform their familiar and deadly head-on attacks. In the always-vulnerable low position, the 388th Bomb Group lost 11 of the 21 B-17s it launched that day. Only one of the combat wings was able to see the target clearly enough to bomb; for the rest of the B-17s, the clouds and smokescreens robbed them of the opportunity, and some 233 bombers looked for opportune targets on the way home. The Luftwaffe continued to attack, and the B-17s of some groups began to run low on gasoline following detours above clouds and, in some cases, multiple bomb runs before a target could be acquired. A dozen Fortresses had to ditch in the English Channel, their fuel exhausted from the extra work over the Continent. Amazingly, all of the crewmen of these B-17s were rescued. Forty-five Fortresses would not return from Stuttgart that day, many due to weather-related fuel-starvation and other complications. The need for reliable electronic means of bombing through overcast was manifest, to avoid debacles like this.

Still, the losses mounted in the fall of 1943 as weather over the Continent cleared and B-17s rose to attack. On 14 October, Schweinfurt was revisited. When the escorting P-47 Thunderbolts reached the end of their duration, they had to return to England, leaving the B-17s vulnerable to attack by successive waves of German fighters. The 138 damaged Fortresses were lucky; 60 of their fellows were downed.[55]

The arithmetic was stunning: Eighth Air Force had lost 148 bombers in a week of operations in the fall of 1943, well over the prohibitive threshold of 10 percent losses that AAF planners used as a guideline. Mastery of the air was absent, especially when escorting Allied fighters had to heed fuel gauges and leave the scene. Eighth Air Force withdrew, temporarily, from the targeting of sites deep in Germany until adequate numbers of long-range fighters could be made available. If shallower raids were dispatched for a while, Eighth Air Force could take comfort in the knowledge that their numbers were steadily growing both in bomber and fighter assets.

As the Eighth Air Force continued to press its point, both with the Germans and with Allied planners who were faced with the unenviable task of parceling out finite resources to a variety of users, it was vital to make every sortie by every bomber count. Mechanical problems resulting in the failure of an aircraft to drop bombs on the target were most vexing. With precise detail, the mighty Eighth Air Force analyzed missions to learn the magnitude and cause of mechanical failures which kept the bombers from doing their job:

This analysis of causes of Heavy Bomber aircraft failing to bomb because of mechanical failure covers 66 operations of VIII Bomber Command from 2 October 1943 to 31 December 1943. Twenty-eight of these operations were carried out during the day and 38 were carried out at night, the latter consisting of night leaflet operations during which one to eight aircraft took off for each operation. 13,567 aircraft took off during the period studied, of which 164 aircraft took off on night operations. The number of aircraft failing mechanically on these night operations were negligible, amounting to only 5 of the total of 1,314 failing mechanically.[56]

In summarizing the findings, the statistical control office of Eighth Air Force noted: "Particular attention is

In the 390th Bomb Group's camera loading room, K-21 aerial cameras were readied for a mission. Tape held covers in place on film magazines; light leaks were common. *(AAF/Jerry Cole.)*

Processing large rolls of aerial strike film was a vital and ongoing chore in bomb groups like the 390th. *(AAF/Jerry Cole.)*

called to the fact that the 2nd Bomb Division (B-24s) reported higher percentages of mechanical incidents than the 1st and 3rd Bomb Divisions (B-17) for both periods studied." The statisticians produced a chart depicting mechanical incidents as a percentage of aircraft taking off for the various divisions for two time periods: 25 June–28 September 1943 and 2 October–31 December 1943:

Mechanical Incidents As Percent of Aircraft Taking Off

	25 June– 28 Sep 43	2 Oct– 31 Dec 43
1st Bomb Division (B-17)	15.0%	9.6%
2nd Bomb Division (B-24)	18.7%	17.6%
3rd Bomb Division (B-17)	11.4%	12.8%

SOURCE: Report, "Analysis of Heavy Bomber Aircraft Failing to Bomb Because of Mechanical Failure, 2 October through 31 December 1943," HQ., USSTAF Statistical Control Office, 26 February 1944.

The B-24 was at a disadvantage. It was several years newer than the B-17 and had been essentially rushed into production and combat without the benefit of lengthy peacetime operations during which to divine its faults, as had the more mature B-17 design. And as the Liberator pushed the state of the art forward, some of its design features were more problem-plagued. There's a quote—possibly apocryphal—attributed to then-Col. Curtis LeMay

A publicity photo suggested a christening of the Eighth Air Force B-17G *Spirit of '44* by pilot First Lt. Eldridge Greer to mark the end of 1943. *(Air Force photo 26848AC.)*

A life-jacketed bombardier peered from the Plexiglas nose of a 490th Bomb Group B-17G returning to England; its day's work finished. *(Brown/USAFA.)*

e original B-17E, first of the big-tailed B-17 variants, was tested
d photographed over the forests and farms of Puget Sound, pre-
ging the din of thousands of wartime Boeing bombers to follow.
eing/Tom Cole.)

Yellow-tailed B-17G of the 839th Bomb Squadron, 487th Bomb Group, held formation with a fellow Fortress from which this Kodachrome slide was made during an unusual fire-bombing mission in April 1945. *(Brown/USAFA.)*

Probably photographed in the first half of 1943, a trio of 91st Bomb Group B-17Fs over England typifies the extensive camouflage of that era of the war. The white national star insignia has been toned down with gray to diminish visibility, and blotchy medium green patches are evident on the nearest aircraft, in an effort to break up the geometric lines of the airframe. (Air Force photo.)

A B-17C in all its prewar glory and shiny splendor rose from the runway at Boeing Field in Seattle, Washington. Versions of the C-model saw early combat with the British as the Fortress I; similar D-models were in use by the AAF early in the Pacific war. (Boeing.)

A tableau played out repeatedly in England during the war s ground crews, some with the bicycles that were so prevalen England, earnestly watching the return of 100th Bomb Group B-2 from a mission. The end of the mission meant work for the mech ics, assessing and patching sheetmetal damage as needed, tending engines that would have to power the bombers safely o the target and back the next time the cycle was replay (Brown/USAFA.)

Its Norden bombsight covered, this Eighth Air Force B-17F in England carried a tribute to V-mail, a high priority communication system instated to facilitate mail between crews and families at home. Late-style cheek gun window used K-5 gun mount for .50-caliber machine gun. *(Brown/USAFA.)*

The 388th Bomb Group put up a mixed fleet of silver and older camouflaged B-17s for a mission to Brest on 26 August 1944. Fortresses were staggered to present the most guns, and the fewest opportunities, to German fighter pilots. *(Brown/USAFA.)*

Viewed from the nose of another B-17 on 26 August 1944, a veteran G-model of the 388th Bomb Group showed evidence of a replacement left outer wing panel. In the rush to keep the bombers airworthy, paint and markings sometimes suffered as mechanics tended to more vital chores on their Fortresses between missions. *(Brown/USAFA.)*

"Lucky Stehley Boy" of the 447th Bomb Group wore its luck in the form of numerous aluminum patches covering battle damage that did not down the Fortress. Stirrup handle visible in top turret dome is gun charging grip. *(Brown/USAFA.)*

We may never know how many bombers named "Queenie" faced the Axis; this 76-mission veteran B-17G photographed in England sported a shamrock that faced forward when the chin turret was stowed to the right. *(Brown/USAFA.)*

The 100th Bomb Group's "Lady Geraldine" discharged its crew, bearing parachute packs and life preservers following a mission. Gray painted chin turrets were not uncommon on natural metal B-17Gs, and probably resulted from a stockpile of prepainted turrets on hand at the time camouflage was discarded on the B-17 assembly line. A curious reversal of the curved cowling paint of earlier camouflaged Fortresses is visible here. The antiglare panel does not reach the lip of the cowling on this example. *(Brown/USAFA.)*

On the first day of the truce for Chow Hound food-dropping missions, photographer Maj. Mark Brown was the subject of this informal portrait beside the roughly sprayed checkertail of a 385th Bomb Group B-17G. Not all warplanes received the meticulous paint and masking associated with postwar restorations. *(Brown/USAFA.)*

A 490th Bomb Group G-model in an incongruously peaceful portrait in England awaited a mission to carry some of the brightly painted bombs to a German target. *(Brown/USAFA.)*

Nose to tail, B-17Gs of the 487th Bomb Group taxied back to parking after a fire bomb mission in mid-April 1945. Broad, bright geometric color panels identified Eighth Air Force bomb units late in the war in an almost contemptuous disregard for German attacks. *(Brown/USAFA.)*

Brightly painted drone B-17G flew perilously close to nuclear blasts in Bikini tests to gather test data in 1946. *(Air Force via Dave Menard.)*

B-17F registration number N17W participated in a fire ant poisoning program in Georgia in 1963 when it temporarily flew out of Dobbins Air Force Base, where it was photographed. One of only a few F-models to reach civilian owners, N17W subsequently became a fire bomber and sometime movie star, with credits including *The Thousand Plane Raid*, *Tora! Tora! Tora!*, and the Hollywood fictionalized feature version of *Memphis Belle*. N17W, a genuine Boeing product, was purchased by Bob Richardson for inclusion in the Museum of Flight in Seattle, Washington. *(Photo by Kenneth G. Johnsen.)*

Radical B-17F conversion to Rolls Royce Dart turboprop engines briefly served as an air tanker in 1970 before crashing while fighting fires that year. Registered N1340N, this Fortress carried call sign 34A as a fire bomber. It was photographed in July 1970 at Wenatchee, Washington during a spate of severe wildfires in north central Washington. *(Photo by Kenneth G. Johnsen.)*

of the B-17 flying 305th Bomb Group that goes: "The B-24 is all right, but it will never replace the airplane." Mechanical statistics such as these may have inspired such talk, and numerous Eighth Air Force documents are flavored with preferences for the B-17 Flying Fortress.

The Mediterranean, 1943

Twelfth Air Force possessed olive drab B-17s with which to target Axis transportation and power-generation facilities in North Africa in January 1943. P-38s were welcome escort fighters in this time period. The 97th and 301st Bomb Groups possessed B-17s as early as November 1942; the 99th and Second Bomb Groups weighed in with 12th Air Force in the spring of 1943; by the end of October, all of these 12th AF Fortress assets would migrate to 15th Air Force, fighting from Italy.

Not only did the North African Fortresses target the Axis on that continent, but on 15 February, 12th Air Force B-17s bombed shipping and the harbor at Palermo. Occasionally that spring, the North African Fortresses cruised between Tunisia and Sicily, hitting Axis shipping they encountered. German and Italian interests were in peril both for their North African excursion as well as for the safety of Sicily and Italy in the upcoming months. On 22 February 1943, B-17s began the first of several missions to bomb the retreating forces of Gen. Rommel at Kasserine Pass and the town of Kasserine.[57]

By early April, the B-17s were hitting targets at Naples. In the following month, the Tunisian campaign closed with the surrender of the Axis commander of forces in Africa, Marshal Messe. Everyone knew that Sicily and Italy would be the next targets of 12th Air Force's B-17s. During this period, the 12th Air Force B-17s, operating with other AAF and RAF units under the umbrella of Northwest African Air Forces (NAAF), occasionally employed their own round-the-clock timetable, with nocturnal British Wellington twin-engine bombers hitting targets at some of the same Italian cities visited by the Forts on the following day.[58]

Messina, important in the upcoming Allied invasion of Sicily, reeled under the impact of 300 tons of bombs dropped by NAAF B-17s on 25 June. By 9 July 1943, the Fortresses were part of a varied NAAF roster attacking Sicilian targets including airfields and radar sites as the Allies worked to secure air superiority for the paratroop and glider assault to follow. On 12 July, the B-17s were employed to bomb railroad bridges at Messina. Though this hardly qualified as the kind of long-reach strategic target in the enemy's rear area that AAF planners had envisioned for the B-17s, it nonetheless served a vital need in support of Allied troops on the ground in Sicily. Seven days later, the Mediterranean Theater Fortresses paid a visit over Rome, dropping

Queenie, a B-17F, served in 12th and then 15th Air Force, accruing scars and smudges for each Mediterranean mission survived. Diamond on tail indicated 99th Bomb Group. *(Dennis Peltier collection.)*

bombs on a railyard in the ancient Italian city. The campaign for Italy would frequently pit the B-17s against Italy's renowned rail system, which was vital to moving Axis material and troops.

There was a price paid by B-17s in the air war over Italy, albeit on a scale smaller than that suffered by Fortress units of the Eighth Air Force operating out of England. For September 1943, 12th Air Force posted 1764 B-17 sorties, losing 12 Fortresses and listing eight more B-17s as missing during that month. By the end of the month, Allied ground forces occupied a significant portion of the southern part of the Italian peninsula.[59]

In the following month, the target list for 12th AF Fortresses would include German airfields on occupied Greece, including Athens and Salonika, as well as bridges in Albania. On the last day of October 1943, 12th Bomb Group B-17s attacked a viaduct at Antheor. The next day, the Fortresses of 12th AF were transferred to the new 15th Air Force. In addition to inheriting the 2d, 97th, 99th, and 301st Bomb Groups and their B-17s, 15th Air Force would, in the spring of 1944, boost its strength with the addition of the 463d and 483d Bomb Groups, flying B-17s until the end of the war. The reach into Germany from the south meant 15th Air Force B-17s based at Foggia could tag some targets not easily attained by their Eighth Air Force counterparts out of England. AAF planners also hoped the more temperate weather of Italy would generate more flying days than the Eighth Air Force could count on in England in the fall and winter months. (Subsequent events would not always bear this out.)

As 1943 played out, 15th Air Force B-17s were used repeatedly against bridges and transportation-related targets. But the Fortresses of the 15th AF also picked off a few targets not usually associated with the air war fought out of Italy, as on 24 November, when B-17s escorted by P-38 fighters attacked the submarine base at Toulon, or again on 2 December 1943, when they targeted sub pens at Marseilles. Even though Allied fighter strength was on the rise, the Luftwaffe could not be counted out, as on 1 December when a force of more than 100 B-17s from 15th Air Force groups bombed the ball bearing works and marshaling yards at Turin. Watchful P-38s engaged German fighters on that mission, with no Lightning losses or victories confirmed. The Fortress gunners, however, put in claims for two enemy fighters shot down. Through the end of the year, 15th Air Force Fortress missions were interspersed among many days of weather-induced stand-downs.[60]

Crushing German Aviation

The heavy losses of Eighth Air Force B-17s and B-24s in 1943 underscored an inescapable fact: The Luftwaffe had to be swept from the skies before the Allies could operate effectively over much of Europe, and this had to take place before any Allied invasion of the Continent could be contemplated. Such a thrust had, almost as an aside, the potential to diminish the German Air Force by downing its fighters when they rose to meet the bomber formations. Codified as Operation Argument in November 1943, the assault on German fighter production capacity was initially stunted by inclement weather. As 1944 dawned, the Eighth Air Force enjoyed growing numbers of B-17s and B-24s as well as improved models of the P-51 Mustang fighter embodying extra internal gasoline tankage plus the ability to carry two underwing tanks for extended range. The P-51 would allow the Fortresses to enjoy fighter escort, in relays, all the way to Berlin and back.[61]

The way in which the AAF would confront the Luftwaffe changed pivotally in January 1944 when Lt. Gen. Jimmy Doolittle, newly named Eighth Air Force commander, drew on his previous experiences in North Africa, where P-38 escort fighters had ranged out ahead of the bomber groups, engaging and disrupting Axis interceptors before the enemy fighters could execute a coordinated attack on the bombers. In England, Doolittle announced a change in fighter tactics to permit escort fighters to precede the bombers as needed to fight the Luftwaffe. On the return flight, if the bombers were secure, escorts could drop down to strafe enemy airfields. The methodology was succinct: No longer did fighters out of

Egg Haid, a B-17G of the 381st Bomb Group in England, showed evidence of ripped canvas chin turret gun slot covers, a problem eventually overcome by using metal strips in the gun slots to baffle the wind. *(Air Force photo.)*

England hug their bombers like armed guards riding shotgun on a stagecoach; now the escorts took the offensive and went seeking combat with the Germans. Doolittle had come to his decision because the Luftwaffe was, correctly from their standpoint, ignoring traditional escorts and pressing attacks on the bombers. If the Germans would not challenge the American fighters, the Americans would have to make the first move.[62]

Operation Argument roared to life over Germany in February 1944, taking advantage of a break in the weather. On 20 February, B-17s and B-24s formed up in their own units to strike several aircraft-manufacturing targets around Leipzig. For the next week—forever known as Big Week—6200 Allied bombing sorties delivered more than 19,000 tons of bombs onto German aircraft- and component-manufacturing plants. British bombers beat up target areas by night, and the Eighth Air Force roared overhead by day. As the RAF posted bomber loss rates of 8 percent and the AAF sustained 6 percent attrition for its daytime raids, the Allies gave up a total of 370 bombers and 38 fighters that week. The Luftwaffe tallied 230 aircraft lost in aerial combat. But even as AAF planners in England were bracing themselves for a war of attrition to snuff out the Luftwaffe, the fruits of Big Week were manifesting themselves: More Mustangs kept arriving in England at a time when German fighters, some carrying experienced warriors, were being downed. And German flight training was already disrupted by the war overhead, unlike AAF training in the peaceful, untouched United States.

For its successes in hurting German manufacturing capacity, Big Week's impact was blunted as Germany continued to decentralize aircraft production. But the engagements with the fielded aircraft of the Luftwaffe were attractive. Eighth Air Force next began a campaign that increased emphasis on destroying the Luftwaffe on the wing instead of in the factory. Now, instead of sending B-17s over relatively safe targets, Eighth Air Force chose to provoke the biggest enemy fighter response possible by sending the heavies over the German capital, Berlin! This agreed with the ideas of Lt. Gen. Carl A. "Tooey" Spaatz, whom Hap Arnold had named commander of the United States Strategic Air Forces (USSTAF) and who had operational control over both 8th and 15th Air Forces. General Spaatz had wanted such a confrontation since December 1943, but the plan was deferred until sufficient long-range escort fighters could be fielded by the AAF to win a grim attrition fight. More AAF fighters than any time previous were launched in support of the bombers over Berlin.

The first Eighth Air Force strike over the German capital involved only 31 B-17s on 4 March 1944, after weather caused many others to divert. During the first part of the so-called Battle of Berlin, German fighters still operated under a constraint that kept them from proactively engaging American fighters, ignoring these to push attacks on the bombers. This had the effect of freeing the AAF fighters to initiate combat with the Germans. Late in March, the Luftwaffe began modifying its battle plans to allow a third of its fighters to attack AAF fighters in a premeditated move to lure them away from the bombers so other fighters could raid the heavies with relative ease. But as German fighter pilots would later recall, the rout was already accomplished by this time. Inexperienced German replacement pilots filled Luftwaffe cockpits, and the once-formidable fighting force was bereft of its corporate knowledge, its heritage of dogfighting finesse. Unit air discipline declined on the German side, and AAF fighters enjoyed numerical superiority as they rampaged among the Messerschmitts and Focke Wulfs.[63]

But the tactic of using bombers over Berlin to draw out the Luftwaffe was not without grave peril for Eighth Air Force. On 6 March 1944, 69 four-engine AAF bombers—the largest loss to date—went down under determined Luftwaffe attacks. Of these, 53 were B-17s and 15 were from the 100th Bomb Group alone. Two days later, the Eighth was back over Berlin and environs, and paid with 36 bombers shot down. On the next day, about 300 B-17s roared over Berlin, using radar to bomb through the overcast. Slight fighter responses were noted, but flak felled nine bombers that day.

The Eighth Air Force was able to recover from the losses of February and March 1944 with new B-17s, B-24s, and new escort fighters. Episodic bomber losses were still occasionally alarming, but the Luftwaffe's fighting edge had been forever dulled. Out of the smoky haze of the battles over Berlin would emerge the two icons of the American air war over Europe: the B-17 Flying Fortress and the P-51 Mustang.

With bomb bay doors open, the bomb load can be discerned in a B-17G high over Europe. Broad bomb doors of B-17s sometimes inadvertently cued the Luftwaffe when the Forts were committed to the bomb run and unable to take evasive action, their bombardiers likely to be busy and unable to man any nose guns. *(SDAM.)*

B-17G 42-102953 of the 388th Bomb Group required a crazy-quilt patchwork of skin repairs. Minor tears in the skin sometimes were deferred until major maintenance could be performed on the airplane if the small holes posed no threat of enlarging. Photo taken 21 June 1944. *(Brown/USAFA.)*

The 91st Bomb Group's *Bomber Dear* was B-17G-45-BO 42-97234. Ladders or scaffolds were necessary to create photos of crewmen juxtaposed with the high noses of B-17s. *(Air Force photo.)*

There was another facet to the Allies' assault on the Luftwaffe. To counter the Germans' ability to evacuate fighters from airfields in the path of daylight strikes once the bomber formation's intentions were known, some fighter bases were visited by the RAF in the predawn darkness, dropping bombs and sowing antipersonnel munitions and other devices intended to hamper the movement of German fighters until after the AAF had a chance to bomb the fields.

Europe: The Long Haul, 1944–1945

The Combined Bomber Offensive with the Royal Air Force drew to a close at the beginning of April 1944, and USSTAF became a tool for Gen. Eisenhower to use in advancing the invasion of the Continent that summer. The heavy bombers participated in a deception that saw targets both inside and outside the Normandy region of France visited by B-17s and B-24s in an effort to keep the real invasion site a mystery as long as possible. Meanwhile, two schools of thought were at odds over the best way to cripple Germany to permit the invasion to progress over the Continent. One group favored bombing German petroleum sources to starve the machinery of war. The other camp argued that this approach would take too long to yield results. The real target of choice, they said, was the transportation system on which Germany depended. Eisenhower opted for targeting transportation, and even the heavies participated. Nonetheless, on 8 June 1944, USSTAF's Gen. Spaatz reminded Eighth and 15th Air Forces that their primary strategic mission remained the destruction of German oil facilities.[64]

The AAF and RAF knew what they had to do to topple the German regime. The two Allied Air Forces brought their varied strategic and tactical might to bear on target systems

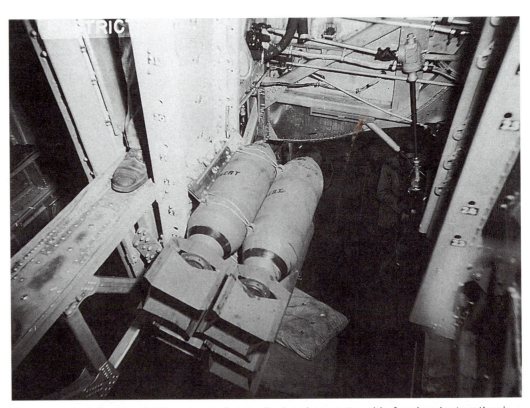

One way to increase the B-17's capacity for smaller bombs was to cable four bombs together in a cluster relying on only one stainless steel shackle attached to the bomb rack, as demonstrated in a 388th Bomb Group Fortress in May 1944. *(Brown/USAFA.)*

A huge secondary explosion roiled upward from the I.G. Farbendustrie chemical plant in Ludwig-shaven as a 92d Bomb Group B-17G passed overhead on 27 May 1944. *(AAF via Keith Laird.)*

In the spring of 1944, about 35,000 war workers at Boeing painted their names on the 5000th Seattle-built B-17, soon to be nicknamed *Five Grand*. It was an auspicious start for a bomber that survived a wheels-up landing in England and combat as part of the 96th Bomb Group. *(Boeing.)*

Five Grand was the subject of a postwar newspaper campaign by the *Seattle Star,* as well as efforts by Seattle city councilman Bob Jones, hoping for memorialization of the milestone B-17G in the city of its birth. Instead, *Five Grand,* wearing fading unit markings over some of its signatures, joined the rows of Fortresses scrapped at Kingman, Arizona, in the immediate postwar years. *(William T. Larkins.)*

The Yankee Doodle Dandy of Hollywood, James Cagney, visited the 390th Bomb Group in England to christen a B-17G of that name. Muzzle flares on chin turret guns may have been applied in an effort to avoid damaging the nose glazing when the guns were fired at extreme upward elevation. *(AAF/Jerry Cole.)*

German defenders unleashed smoke warfare to obscure the target and recognition features in an effort to deny Eighth Air Force the opportunity for visual bombing as 91st BG B-17Gs approached. *(SDAM.)*

including transportation and oil, while still checking the Luftwaffe in the skies, bombing V-1 sites in occupied countries, and up to the June invasion, softening up German defenses on the coast of France. B-17s were a part of the brew that spelled an increasingly palpable impending defeat of Germany.

The invasion on 6 June 1944 included waves totaling more than 1000 B-17s and B-24s attacking German defenses before troops went ashore. For once, Pathfinder radar planes accompanied the heavies over occupied Normandy instead of relegating their electronic efforts to Germany.

Even with attacks on Axis oil as well as transportation choke points, the Germans were proving adept at producing trucks well into 1944, prompting attacks on specific truck factories.

A longstanding wish of AAF planners had been to gain access to airfields in the Soviet Union from which to stage heavy bomber missions. As early as October 1942, requests had been made for allowing heavy bombers to land in Russia upon completion of long-range strikes at German targets. On 2 June 1944, the idea bore fruit when B-17s assigned to units of the 15th Air Force rolled out from bombing marshaling yards at Debreczen, Hungary, bringing 70 P-51s with them all the way into the Soviet Union for recovery at Poltava and Mirgorod. The Fortresses rose from their Soviet fields again on 6 June 1944, striking at a Romanian airfield before again returning to Russia.

One of the fliers on the first shuttle effort, First Lt. Clifton Ackerman of the 97th Bomb Group, gave a

An airman and a Russian soldier shared a cigarette by the nose of a B-17G nicknamed *I Dood It* during a shuttle mission. *(Air Force photo.)*

Soviet soldiers used brooms to sweep the ramp at a Russian shuttle base, with a 390th Bomb Group B-17G parked behind them. *(Bowman collection.)*

detailed postmission briefing. He said ground crews prepared for the mission for more than 2 weeks in secrecy, readying the Fortresses of four bomb groups. "It was highly obvious that something was in the air," Lieutenant Ackerman said, ". . . for each day we could see the other groups going out or hear them going out in the morning and returning in the afternoon from a mission." The crews were briefed about the mission on 1 June 1944. "We learned that we would carry with us fighter equipment and supplies, medical supplies and field rations to last us some two days," the lieutenant explained. "We turned in early that night and on the morning of June Second went in for our final briefing. In our final briefing we were given identification cards, our phrase books, a passport stating our name, that we were American airmen, and it also listed Russian and American phrases in case we did go down outside of our Russian base . . ."[65]

Bomb load was restricted to only five 500-lb general purpose bombs per Fortress to allow for the carriage of supplies for this expeditionary force. As the bombers and their AAF P-51 escort droned on to their Soviet landing fields, some crews reported seeing Russian fighters flying along with the flotilla near the Soviet–German front lines, about 150 to 200 mi from Poltava. Once over Russian territory, the Fortresses were to let down to 7000 ft. When inclement weather littered the route at that altitude, the 97th Bomb Group let down still lower over the flat terrain, taking its 21 big bombers across Russia at no more than 2500 ft, according to Lieutenant Ackerman's account. "We could see people working on the farms. We could see people repairing their homes . . . that had been damaged due to the terrific amount of battling that had gone on back and forth in this area." At about 4:30 that afternoon, the Forts reached Poltava. As they taxied to parking, the B-17s were guided by jeeps around bomb craters, although a few Fortresses broke through the surface nonetheless.[66]

The fliers were greeted by a small contingent of Americans in place to service the planes and see to any medical needs. "There was approximately one [American] man per aircraft, and somewhere between four or five Russian assistants . . . It was their job to repair battle damage, make engine changes and the necessary work to be done on the airplanes," Lieutenant Ackerman explained. The shuttle-bomber crews were put up in a tent city at Poltava, he said. In preparation for the 6 June strike on the Romanian airfield, Lieutenant Ackerman said, "Each crew had to load their own bombs, with the assistance of Russian soldiers." This time, it was 250-pounders the men shackled into the tight bomb bays of the Fortresses, taking a half day as the Americans and Russians worked through a vast gulf of language differences.[67]

The 6 June mission to Romania encountered meager flak and no enemy fighters. After the mission, German reconnaissance aircraft made inroads at night over the B-17s' base in Russia, Lieutenant Ackerman said. "Out of the three reconnaissance planes that came to our field alone, two of them were shot down—one by antiaircraft fire and one by fighters." Lieutenant Ackerman was sure the German intruders had succeeded in getting photos of the field. He said plans had called for the 15th Air Force B-17s to stage a couple more shuttle missions out of the Soviet Union, but the supply of bombs was not adequate to permit this. The final effort was an 11 June mission, with the Fortresses bound for Italy after making one more strike. Lieutenant Ackerman's Fortress took flak hits on that mission that ultimately incapacitated two of his B-17's Wright Cyclones, necessitating a return to Poltava. Now isolated from the rest of the bombers, this Fort was not repaired until about 10 days later, at which time the Soviets insisted it could only leave Russian airspace with an escort provided by a Russian pilot, navigator, and radio operator in a Soviet airplane, pacing the Fortress as far as Tehran.[68]

The shuttle option was exercised by Eighth Air Force on 21 June 1944 as 123 B-17s hit a synthetic oil plant at Ruhland while 22 more Fortresses dropped on other targets. One Fortress was lost that day; the other 144, split into groups of 73 and 71 bombers, landed at Poltava and Mirgorod, respectively. The B-17s enjoyed American P-47 and then P-51 escorts in shifts all the way into Russia. But the relative ease of the mission vanished in the startling glare of German flares over Poltava that night as nocturnal Luftwaffe bombers destroyed 47 B-17s on the ground and damaged still more. More than a dozen P-51s were written off. Stored gasoline and ammunition at that Soviet field were also hit. The surviving B-17s moved farther east into the Soviet Union for safekeeping as they replenished themselves for the return one-way bombing mission. Soviet cooperation did not extend to allowing American fighters to defend their temporary airfields. By 26 June 1944, 72 repaired or unscathed B-17s from Poltava and Mirgorod, escorted by 55 P-51s from Piryatin, rose from their Soviet bases to bomb another oil refinery, this time at Drohobycz. The American warplanes then recovered at Foggia in Italy before migrating back to England. If the shuttle-bombing concept had merit, the high losses experienced by Eighth Air Force were

German flak threw hot steel splinters at 351st BG B-17Gs winging over a few cotton clouds. *(Don Whittaker collection.)*

With a chin-mounted search radar, B-17Hs were converted G-models slinging a lifeboat that could be airdropped to downed aircrews if other forms of rescue were too distant. The modified Fortresses later were redesignated SB-17Gs. *(Author collection.)*

The black Y in a white square, plus the 4 on the tail, mark this as a 301st Bomb Group veteran. When the 15th Air Force put formations of B-17s over the Alps en route from Italy to Germany, the prevalent mud of Italian airfields coated the bombers' undersides and froze at altitude. Some 15th Air Force B-17 ball turret gunners stretched condoms over the muzzles of their turret guns to keep mud and debris out during taxiing and takeoff. *(Don Hayes collection.)*

nonetheless troublesome.[69] Hampered by a less than perfect partnership with some of the Soviets, shuttle bombing did not blossom, and American hopes for basing three AAF heavy bomb groups inside Russia died late that year.

The German army offensive in the Ardennes in the winter of 1944 was met with a continuation of sorties against transportation targets. Momentarily, Generals Arnold and Spaatz were taken aback by Germany's evident resilience in the face of continued strategic and tactical bombing, although the Ardennes offensive was broken by the Allies. In fact, this late effort by the Germans was only made possible by the expenditure of hoarded resources that could no longer be replenished.[70]

Oil and transportation continued to dominate the B-17 calendar of targets into 1945. In at least one instance, Eighth Air Force B-17s responded to a Soviet request for help on the eastern front by targeting a German rail center at Oranienburg. The unrelenting pace of B-17 missions actually resulted in a dearth of true strategic targets in Germany by the end of April 1945. Within days, German officials were grasping the shattered remnants of their nation in the aftermath of Hitler's suicide. They surrendered on 7 May 1945.

Flopping a flattened right main tire, a 99th Bomb Group, 15th Air Force, B-17G used a crew parachute to slow its landing roll because brakes and the electrical system were also out of commission, circa October 1944. *(AAF photo.)*

Up from Italy, 1944–1945

The ability of the AAF to mount heavy bomber attacks against Axis targets from Italy as well as from England effectively opened a two-front air war against the Germans, the intensity of which only increased in 1944 and 1945 as the strengths of both the 8th and 15th Air Forces continued to grow. During 1944, the number of B-24 groups in 15th Air Force would outstrip the number of B-17 units there; six Fortress groups in 15th Air Force would eventually be augmented by 15 B-24 Liberator groups operating out of Italy. In 1944 and 1945, 8th and 15th Air Forces would be the bastions of the Flying Fortresses.

Ground fighting in Italy was intense and belabored. When German forces holed up in the Benedictine abbey at Monte Cassino, one result was the targeting of the abbey on 15 February 1944 by about 100 15th Air Force B-17s as well as by B-25 and B-26 medium bombers of 12th Air Force. Two days later, B-17s and B-24s of 15th Air Force bombed truck parks and troop concentrations in the Anzio vicinity, as Allied ground forces there were under heavy counterattack from the Germans. Fifteenth Air Force Fortresses hit an aircraft factory at Steyr and a petroleum refinery at Fiume on 24 February, coordinating these moves with Eighth Air Force heavy bomber efforts against Germany, especially its aircraft industrial plant.[71]

The lure of the Ploesti oil fields was too great to ignore in 1944 as American bomber strength grew and as bases were acquired closer to Ploesti. In August 1943, masses of B-24 Liberators had reached Ploesti from Libya in a one-shot raid that hurt production of petroleum for a while but could not neutralize Ploesti as a prime producer of petroleum products for the German military. Now, 8 months later, 15th Air Force took up the cudgel with a 5 April 1944 mission to Ploesti involving a total of 334 B-17s and B-24s. Enemy fighters and antiaircraft batteries accounted for a total of 13 heavy bombers downed on that strike.[72]

White radome in place of a ball turret identifies this B-17G-VE 44-8020 as a 15th Air Force Pathfinder. A small window in the radio room has been blanked on this aircraft, possibly to improve the radar operator's ability to see scope. *(Don Hayes collection.)*

A crewmember of this 97th Bomb Group B-17G danced for joy with a mechanic in Italy after a grueling mission over Germany. For many, the greatest gift was simply to survive another day. *(Don Hayes collection.)*

Between 5 April and 19 August 1944, 15th Air Force developed a Ploesti campaign that embraced 20 missions there (including one by bomb-laden P-38s). Fortresses flew on more than a dozen of the Ploesti missions in the oil campaign of 1944. By 30 August, advancing Soviet forces occupied Ploesti, taking it out of the war once and for all. The next day, in a curious scene involving former combatants, more than three dozen 15th Air Force B-17s landed at Bucharest, Romania, to repatriate some 1000 American airmen who had been shot down during the Romanian oil raids.[73]

The Luftwaffe's use of cannon-armed jet-powered Me-262s posed a serious threat to the bombers. On 24 March 1945, 15th Air Force dispatched more than 150 Fortresses to hit a tank works in Berlin. Flak claimed some B-17s that day, but the sharklike Messerschmitt jets ripped other Forts from the skies over the German capital. Fifteenth Air Force B-17 gunners put in claims for Me-262s shot down in the same gun battle. The Fortresses of 15th Air Force completed their wartime exploits with a marshaling yard attack over Salzburg on 1 May 1945.

Fortresses, Food, and Freedom

If the suspension of civility that war imposes is unsettling, occasional episodes of compassion in combat are even more stunning. In 1864, when stiff fighting between Union and Confederate forces near Marietta, Georgia, ignited the pine woods, both sides agreed to a truce while they evacuated the wounded from the path of the flames. Then, the killing resumed.

More than 80 years later, portions of Holland lay in shambles, with battle-scars and floods exacerbating a lack of food. This held dire consequences of famine for Dutch civilians. German occupiers in the west, though cut off by British and Canadian troops, still had some fight in them. Through neutral channels, a remarkable truce took shape in the last few days before the war ended. The Third Division was tasked to airdrop emergency rations at low level over Holland. The B-17s involved in these "Chow Hound" missions were given specific routes and drop zones, outside of which it was still wartime as usual. Starting 1 May 1945 and running daily except on 4 May, the Fortresses skimmed over towns and farms at 500 ft, dropping sacks of flour and GI rations at The Hague and near Rotterdam. Germans and Dutch looked up as the big bombers, sometimes in tight formations, roared overhead. Hundreds of sorties were flown each day. Only one incident of antiaircraft fire was noted, and this may have happened because of inadvertent flight outside the truce corridors.[74]

Through the course of the war in Europe, from August 1942 to May 1945, the Eighth Air Force's two heavy bombers, the B-17 and B-24, had a total loss to flak of 2439 aircraft, while Axis fighters accounted for 2452 of both types of bombers, a count too close to call, although the losses to each kind of enemy peril varied from month to month. For Eighth Air Force B-17s and B-24s combined, the high point in losses due to fighters came in April 1944 when 314 heavies were shot down. The high point in Eighth Air Force flak losses of B-17s and B-24s came in August 1944 when 238 four-engine American bombers were downed by antiaircraft fire. In the Mediterranean Theater of Operations (MTO) between June 1942 and May 1945, 847 B-17s and B-24s succumbed to enemy fighters, and 1313 were downed by antiaircraft fire. High combined B-17 and B-24 loss to Axis fighters in the MTO came in February 1944 as 106 heavies of both types were shot down by fighters. High MTO losses of B-17s and B-24s to antiaircraft fire came in July 1944 with 170 of both types of heavy bombers downed by groundfire. By 1945, losses to Eighth and 15th Air Force heavy bombers were more likely to come from antiaircraft fire than from the ravaged Luftwaffe's fighters, although remarkably, in April 1945, German fighters downed 72 Eighth Air Force B-17s and B-24s combined.[75]

A startlingly incongruous-looking portrait by Jerome Cole of the 390th Bomb Group, taken from his perch in a B-17 ball turret, showed Germans atop a flak tower in Holland observing a truce as food-bearing Fortresses roared low overhead in early May 1945. The shadow of one of the B-17s eclipsed the flak tower symbolically, for the war was all but over. *(AAF photo by Jerry Cole.)*

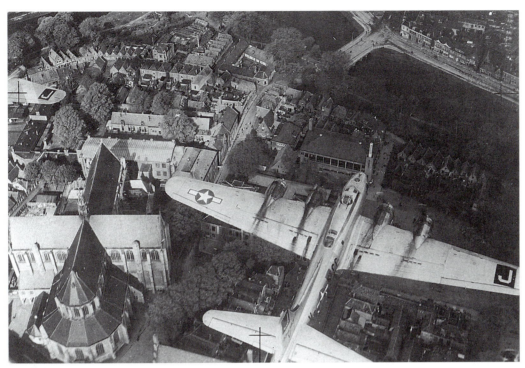

A cathedral and row houses in Holland reverberated under the thunder of low-flying B-17Gs of the 390th Bomb Group, bringing emergency famine relief supplies in early May 1945. *(AAF photo by Jerry Cole.)*

Epilogue

The Army Air Forces' Flying Fortresses flew combat for only 4 years, yet etched their image into the tableau of history. The great bombing-experiment over Europe will never be repeated in the fashion of World War II, and the successes and failures of the B-17's war against Germany must forever stand as they are. Had more B-17s been available earlier, the war might have been carried deep into Germany sooner. Detractors of the AAF's campaigns over Europe tend to point out how well Germany fought into 1945. Yet the efforts of

Bundles of food and flour rained down on Holland the first few days of May 1945 as Chow Hound missions brought relief to the endangered area under an unusual truce between Germany and the United States. *(390th BG/Jerry Cole.)*

Trucked in pieces through the streets of Paris, a brace of B-17Gs was assembled beneath the Eiffel Tower for a victory celebration. Natural metal Fortress carried the 94th Bomb Group's A in a black rectangle on its yellow vertical fin. In the photo, a B-24 Liberator awaited reassembly as well. *(Photo by Frank W. Laird via Keith Laird.)*

Men of the 390th Bomb Group held the victory edition of *Stars and Stripes* proclaiming Germany's defeat, clutched pets, and grinned as they posed for a celebratory victory photograph in May 1945. Combat photographer Jerome "Jerry" Cole, near the center of the photo, held his calico mouser cat, Mabel, who seemed disinterested in the monumental turn of human events. *(Jerry Cole collection.)*

the fleets of B-17s forced Germany to divert resources to air defense and to dispersal of key industries, effectively dissipating a measure of strength from that country's war effort.

Without the B-17s' contributions, what would the outcome have looked like? Some points are unarguable: The B-17 was thrown into the thick of battle in the harshest combat arena of World War II, where it earned the preference of leaders such as Gen. Jimmy Doolittle. And the B-17 crews, like their B-24 counterparts, fought with all the determination, courage, passion, pride, ingenuity, and humor that Americans are proud to claim as a cultural personality.

Notes

1. George W. Gray, *Frontiers of Flight—The Story of NACA Research*, Alfred A. Knopf, New York, N.Y., 1948.
2. *Army Air Forces Statistical Digest, World War II*, Office of Statistical Control, HQ, USAAF, December 1945.
3. Kit C. Carter and Robert Mueller, compilers, *Combat Chronology, 1941–1945, U.S. Army Air Forces in World War II*, Center for Air Force History, Washington, D.C., 1991.
4. *Ibid.*
5. *Ibid.*
6. Interview, Frederick A. Johnsen with Gen. Brooke Allen, USAF (Ret.), circa 1977, and Kit C. Carter and Robert Mueller, compilers, *Combat Chronology, 1941–1945, U.S. Army Air Forces in World War II*, Center for Air Force History, Washington, D.C., 1991.
7. Kenn C. Rust, *Seventh Air Force Story*, Historical Aviation Album, Temple City, Calif., 1979.
8. Barrett Tillman, *The Dauntless Dive Bomber of World War Two*, Naval Institute Press, Annapolis, Md., 1976.
9. Memo, from HQ AAF to Chief of Air Staff, Subject: Participation of the Army Air Forces in the Midway Action, 20 June 1942 (filed at AFHRA).
10. *History of the Fifth Bomb Group*, written by members of the unit, published by Hillsborough House, and printed by Commercial Printing Company, Raleigh, N.C., 1946.
11. *Ibid.*
12. *Army Air Forces Statistical Digest, World War II*, Office of Statistical Control, HQ, USAAF, December 1945.
13. George C. Kenney, *General Kenney Reports*, Duell, Sloan, and Pearce, New York, N.Y., 1949.
14. "Oscars vs. B-17," *Air Forces General Information Bulletin*, No. 14, Assistant Chief of Air Staff, Intelligence, Washington, D.C., August 1943.
15. Steve Birdsall, "Special Delivery," *Winged Majesty—The Boeing B-17 Flying Fortress in War and Peace*, Bomber Books, Tacoma, Wash., 1980.
16. "Airborne Lifeboats," *Air Intelligence Digest*, No. 4, 15 August 1945, HQ, AAF Center, Directorate of Operations and Training, Combat Intelligence Branch, Orlando, Fla.
17. Kit C. Carter and Robert Mueller, compilers, *Combat Chronology, 1941–1945, U.S. Army Air Forces in World War II*, Center for Air Force History, Washington, D.C., 1991.
18. *Ibid.*
19. Attributed to a message from Arnold to Portal, April 1942, 8th AF Hq AG files, cited in Hugh Odishaw, "Radar Bombing in the 8th Air Force," under the supervision of the Radiation Laboratory Historical Office, 1946.
20. Hugh Odishaw, "Radar Bombing in the 8th Air Force," under the supervision of the Radiation Laboratory Historical Office, 1946.
21. Kit C. Carter and Robert Mueller, compilers, *Combat Chronology, 1941–1945, U.S. Army Air Forces in World War II*, Center for Air Force History, Washington, D.C., 1991.

22. *Target: Germany—The Army Air Forces' Official Story of the VIII Bomber Command's First Year Over Europe, Life* and Simon and Schuster, New York, N.Y., 1943.

23. *Ibid.*

24. *Ibid.*

25. Wesley Frank Craven and James Lea Cate, editors, *The Army Air Forces in World War II*, imprint by the Office of Air Force History, Washington, D.C., 1983.

26. *Ibid.*

27. Annex No. 3 to Bolero Training Directive—Airplane Loading List [355.02 (Bolero)], HQ, Air Forces Foreign Service Concentration Command, 1 August 1943.

28. *Ibid.*

29. Frederick A. Johnsen, *62nd Military Airlift Wing—Making the History of Air Mobility, 1940–1991,* 62d Airlift Wing History Office, 1992.

30. Wesley Frank Craven and James Lea Cate, editors, *The Army Air Forces in World War II*, imprint by the Office of Air Force History, Washington, D.C., 1983.

31. *Target: Germany—The Army Air Forces' Official Story of the VIII Bomber Command's First Year Over Europe, Life* and Simon and Schuster, New York, N.Y., 1943.

32. Richard G. Davis, *Carl A. Spaatz and the Air War in Europe,* Center for Air Force History, Washington, D.C., 1993.

33. Kenn C. Rust, *Eighth Air Force Story,* Historical Aviation Album, Temple City, Calif., 1978.

34. Kit C. Carter and Robert Mueller, compilers, *Combat Chronology, 1941–1945, U.S. Army Air Forces in World War II,* Center for Air Force History, Washington, D.C., 1991.

35. Roger A. Freeman, *The Mighty Eighth—A History of the U.S. 8th Army Air Force,* Doubleday, Garden City, N.Y., 1970.

36. Kit C. Carter and Robert Mueller, compilers, *Combat Chronology, 1941–1945, U.S. Army Air Forces in World War II,* Center for Air Force History, Washington, D.C., 1991.

37. *Ibid.*

38. A. Timothy Warnock, *Air Power versus U-boats—Confronting Hitler's Submarine Menace in the European Theater,* Air Force History and Museums Program, Washington, D.C., 1999.

39. Hugh Odishaw, "Radar Bombing in the 8th Air Force," under the supervision of the Radiation Laboratory Historical Office, 1946.

40. *Ibid.*

41. *Ibid.*

42. *Ibid.*

43. *Ibid.*

44. Kit C. Carter and Robert Mueller, compilers, *Combat Chronology, 1941–1945, U.S. Army Air Forces in World War II,* Center for Air Force History, Washington, D.C., 1991.

45. Attributed to a message from Eaker to Lovett, 15 December 1943, 8th AF Hq AG files, cited in Hugh Odishaw, "Radar Bombing in the 8th Air Force," under the supervision of the Radiation Laboratory Historical Office, 1946.

46. *Ibid.*

47. Attributed to a message from Eaker to Lovett, 13 December 1943, 8th AF Hq AG files, cited in Hugh Odishaw, "Radar Bombing in the 8th Air Force," under the supervision of the Radiation Laboratory Historical Office, 1946.

48. Hugh Odishaw, "Radar Bombing in the 8th Air Force," under the supervision of the Radiation Laboratory Historical Office, 1946.

49. *Ibid.*

50. *Bombardiers' Information File,* AAF Form 24B, updated March 1945.

51. *Ibid.*

52. Hugh Odishaw, "Radar Bombing in the 8th Air Force," under the supervision of the Radiation Laboratory Historical Office, 1946.
53. Kit C. Carter and Robert Mueller, compilers, *Combat Chronology, 1941–1945, U.S. Army Air Forces in World War II,* Center for Air Force History, Washington, D.C., 1991.
54. Roger A. Freeman, *The Mighty Eighth—A History of the U.S. 8th Army Air Force,* Doubleday, Garden City, N.Y., 1970.
55. Edward T. Russell, *Leaping the Atlantic Wall—Army Air Forces Campaigns in Western Europe, 1942–1945,* Air Force History and Museums Program, Washington, D.C., 1999.
56. Report, "Analysis of Heavy Bomber Aircraft Failing to Bomb Because of Mechanical Failure, 2 October through 31 December 1943," HQ., USSTAF Statistical Control Office, 26 February 1944.
57. Kit C. Carter and Robert Mueller, compilers, *Combat Chronology, 1941–1945, U.S. Army Air Forces in World War II,* Center for Air Force History, Washington, D.C., 1991.
58. *Ibid.*
59. Kenn C. Rust, *Twelfth Air Force Story,* Historical Aviation Album, Temple City, Calif., 1975.
60. Kit C. Carter and Robert Mueller, compilers, *Combat Chronology, 1941–1945, U.S. Army Air Forces in World War II,* Center for Air Force History, Washington, D.C., 1991.
61. R. Cargill Hall, editor, *Case Studies in Strategic Bombardment,* Air Force History and Museums Program, Washington, D.C., 1998.
62. *Ibid.*
63. *Ibid.*
64. Edward T. Russell, *Leaping the Atlantic Wall—Army Air Forces Campaigns in Western Europe, 1942–1945,* Air Force History and Museums Program, Washington, D.C., 1999.
65. First Lt. Clifton Ackerman, "Shuttle Bombing to Russia," Briefing paper, 4 April 1945, preserved by AFHRA.
66. *Ibid.*
67. *Ibid.*
68. *Ibid.*
69. Frederick A. Johnsen, *Boeing B-17 Flying Fortress,* Specialty Press, North Branch, Minn., 1997.
70. Edward T. Russell, *Leaping the Atlantic Wall—Army Air Forces Campaigns in Western Europe, 1942–1945,* Air Force History and Museums Program, Washington, D.C., 1999.
71. Kit C. Carter and Robert Mueller, compilers, *Combat Chronology, 1941–1945, U.S. Army Air Forces in World War II,* Center for Air Force History, Washington, D.C., 1991.
72. *Ibid.*
73. Kenn C. Rust, *Fifteenth Air Force Story,* Historical Aviation Album, Temple City, Calif., 1976.
74. Roger A. Freeman, *The Mighty Eighth—A History of the U.S. Eighth Army Air Force,* Doubleday, Garden City, N.Y., 1970.
75. *Army Air Forces Statistical Digest, World War II,* Office of Statistical Control, HQ, USAAF, December 1945.

The Human Element

People Animated the B-17

Sure, they mellowed somewhat with the passage of years since they rode freezing B-17s over Nazi-held Europe. They became businessmen, fathers, grandfathers, a cross-section of American society eager to see what was around the next bend in their nation's unfurling road to the future. And yet, in the decades that followed victory, all it took was to hear the throbbing sound of radial aircraft engines, feel the coolness in the broad shadow beneath a retired B-17's wings, or listen to a few muffled bars of a Glenn Miller melody to bring back memories of that time when they met and bested a technologically amazing Germany 5 mi above the earth.

Their stories are poignant, funny, rollicking, and sobering, just as the rapid-fire events of their combat lives were. They made leaps of faith to presume they could succeed and survive the war. And they bet their lives on the B-17 Flying Fortress.

SSgt. Richard E. Bowman, Ball Turret Gunner

Years after the war, Richard E. Bowman's countenance tended toward a perpetual smile, a subtle signal that seemed to telegraph patience and peace. Dick Bowman was air-minded, like the name applied to so many in his generation of kids growing up in the 1920s and 1930s. He was an early Aviation Explorer in the Boy Scouts back home in St. Anthony, Idaho. Bowman's demonstrated interest helped land him a slot in the Civilian Pilot Training (CPT) program underway in Pocatello, Idaho. Even as he was being taught the fundamentals of powered planes, Dick Bowman and some of his CPT classmates were cleaved off and placed in glider training programs because the United States at war was continually adjusting its flow of trained military personnel to meet evolving needs. When that particular glider program was subsequently canceled, Bowman recalled, he was given the choice of joining the infantry or going to an Army Air Forces technical school. "I was a little guy; I only weighed 120 pounds," he explained. Though his stature might not have suited him to ground fighting, Bowman was long on spirit and conviction, and he went through aircraft radio training followed by gunnery school at Tyndall Field, Florida.[1]

Richard E. Bowman, second from left, back row, trained on early B-17Gs in Texas before entering combat. *(Richard E. Bowman collection.)*

Gunnery school held some bright moments for Dick Bowman, who grew up around shotguns and duck hunting in his native Idaho. "It actually turned out that if you knew how to shoot skeet, you could shoot airplanes," he said. One of the student gunners' drills involved riding in the back of a jostling stakebed truck over a course at Tyndall and shooting on the run at skeet flung in the air as the truck passed. The gunners were also exposed to the intricacies of tracking skeet with a ball turret fitted with two shotguns.

After he was deemed qualified as an aerial gunner, Dick Bowman was sent to Pyote, Texas, in February 1944, for phase training, where he would meet up with his crew and with a B-17 for the first time. Dick remembered his desire to be assigned to Flying Fortresses: "I wanted to be on a B-17; that was the most talked-about airplane," he said. And of his first flight aboard a Fortress, Dick said: "I was just thrilled," even though the instructor pilot had to leave the landing gear down as a safety precaution on the old weary training B-17 because it might not extend if he retracted it. The old Forts at Pyote "had quite a few hours on them," Dick remembered. The aircraft were essentially F-models upgraded with chin turrets to G-configuration, he said.[2]

Dick's aircraft commander cultivated the crew and decided where to place some members. Bowman's marksmanship, and his size, suggested him for the lower ball turret commanding the approaches to the Fortress from the lower hemisphere beneath the bomber. From then on, the drill consisted of Fortress flights over the wild west as fixed ground targets resembling tanks, trucks, and airplanes hove into view. Sometimes, the drill involved firing at target sleeves towed by another aircraft. And there were the brightly marked P-39 Airacobra fighters that made pursuit passes on the bombers during missions when neither aircraft carried ammunition, allowing the gunners to track a combat aircraft and learn to predict where it would be when their imagined bullets intercepted its path. "I think that helped a lot," said Bowman, the veteran bird hunter.

It was early June when Bowman and his crew left Pyote for Kearney Army Airfield, Nebraska, where new crews and new B-17s were introduced for the flight to Europe. Bowman and his crewmates were filled with enthusiasm at Kearney: "What a feeling that was! We really felt we were about to accomplish something." From Kearney, they guided a shiny new silver B-17G, serial 44-6172, east over the farm fields of Nebraska and into a hailstorm so severe that it damaged oil coolers, dinged the wings as if by a ball-peen hammer, and ripped the zippered canvas wind baffles out of the chin turret gun slots. This new B-17G was one American avenging angel that would have to stop in Bangor, Maine, for repairs before resuming the flight to Gander, Newfoundland.

Dick Bowman and his crew brought their Fortress in to Valley, Wales, on 3 June 1944. They were delayed from going to their base until the first few days after D-Day, 6 June 1944, because all of England was going full-tilt to serve the invasion. Then, by about 8 or 9 June, Bowman and his crewmates took their new bomber to a B-17 pool, where the neophyte crew was summarily separated from this Fortress. "They took us by truck to Snetterton Heath, the 96th Bomb Group, and we flew a few airplanes . . . until a new airplane came in that was assigned to us." It was not unusual for new crews to ferry new B-17s to England, only to be separated from their gleaming new bombers upon arrival. The reasons were varied. Typically, new arriving Fortresses needed some in-country modifications before they were considered compatible for Eighth Air Force purposes, and some bomb groups tended to break in new crews on old airplanes. It seemed to be good stewardship of resources.

Bowman flew on a few training missions in England as the 96th Bomb Group made sure he and his crewmates were tuned in to the way the 96th conducted the business of war. He started his combat career on the 96th Group's B-17 nicknamed "Bad Penny." "It was really war weary," Dick said. The 96th Bomb Group put Bowman's plane in tail-end low positions in formation for a while, he said, because in this slot a new crew was less likely to mess up the rest of a good bombing formation if they failed to hold good position.

When the 96th Bomb Group was tasked to supply B-17s for the 21 June 1944 shuttle bombing mission to a synthetic oil plant at Ruhland, with recovery at Poltava in the Soviet Union, Dick Bowman stepped up for his mandatory yellow fever shot, only to be felled by its side effects along with two of his crewmates, keeping them from the historic shuttle effort.

Dick Bowman's introduction to combat on 24 June 1944 "was kind of a rough mission. We had some mechanical trouble." Right after releasing bombs over Bremen, Dick remembered, "We were well above 20,000 feet and dived rather suddenly, pulling out at about 15,000 feet." From his capsule beneath the belly of the bomber, Bowman was isolated from what was going on in the cockpit. Now separated from the rest of the 96th Bomb Group, Bowman's Fortress tracked across Germany and occupied Holland all alone, a little dot in a big sky. "It was nerve-wracking being all alone," Dick elaborated. As all new airmen were subjected to stories once they arrived at an Eighth Air Force base, Bowman said he had been admonished "you were going to get it if you were a straggler." The ride back to the coast went unchallenged, though, and Snetterton Heath received the returning warriors, somewhat tempered and humbled by their baptism of fire. Bowman said that two of his initial crewmates, profoundly shaken by the events of their first combat sortie, asked to be removed from flight status, a request which he said was honored, with no stigma attached, as combat crews sorted themselves out for the long haul ahead.

Bowman said the first mission "kind of took the bravado out of us and settled us down." As did the subsequent realization that "when we moved into our barracks at Snetterton Heath, it didn't occur to us that we were there because another crew . . . went down."

Barred from riding in the ball turret during takeoff and landing, Bowman did spend most of his time aloft in the small capsule. "As soon as we got over the Channel we were in the turrets. We'd test fire our guns over the Channel," he said. On the return leg, "You'd be in the turret until you were almost over the coast of England before you got out." On a long mission, Dick could count on riding 8 hours in the ball turret. During some missions where the waist gunners expended ammunition, turbulence could bounce spent casings and links into the exposed gear track of Bowman's ball turret, locking him in place until another crewman took a screwdriver and pried the debris clear, he explained.

During his tenure in the skies over Europe, Dick Bowman encountered very little interception by the Luftwaffe, due in part to the enemy's declining numbers in the face of ever-more potent Allied fighter escort capabilities. The few German fighters he encountered came in singly or in pairs. On 2 November 1944, over Merseberg, Dick Bowman rolled his ball turret to meet the attack of an FW-190. Bowman squeezed out ribbons of .50-caliber fire that he said downed the Luftwaffe attacker, although Dick did not receive official credit for the victory. The fighter kill tally process was fraught with pitfalls as mission debriefers tried to sort out claims by several gunners for the same fighter. Confirmation was sometimes hard to come by in the heat of battle.[3]

Though Bowman had been briefed about the existence of the twin-turbojet Me-262 fighter, the presence of the radical rocket-powered Me-163 Komet came as a complete surprise. His perch in the lower ball turret afforded the ideal seat to the spectacle: "We saw an Me-163 . . . come all the way up from the ground with a white column of smoke, and come down through the formation, but it didn't do anything." The almost vertical ascent of the Komet was "very spectacular" to Bowman.

Other sights from Bowman's ball turret were equally surreal. Sometimes, on the return flight to England, he could spot a German V-1 buzz bomb sputtering blindly along in the same general direction, overtaking his Fortress, but out of gun range, like some stylized witch from *The Wizard of Oz*, intent on a mission of mayhem.

If fighters were not the menace they once were by 1944, flak was still ever present. Often, Bowman said his B-17 came back to Snetterton Heath with punctures. Long after a burst of flak had spent its initial violent energy, jagged scraps of shrapnel raining out of the sky still easily punched through the aluminum skins and fabric control surfaces of the B-17s. By that time, repair crews sometimes let dollar-size holes in the metal wait until the Fortress was down for other maintenance, Dick said, and a B-17 might fly missions for a couple of weeks with small perforations picked up along the way.[4]

Bastille Day, 14 July 1944, held significance for the French. So it was with a sense of drama and Allied fraternity that, on this day, the 96th Bomb Group participated in Cadillac Series Three, the name for an operation to airdrop supplies to the French resistance fighters, the Maquis. Dick Bowman recalled taking off at about one or two in the morning for this effort. "We flew low . . . and went down into southern France," he said, looking in the inky darkness for prearranged patterns of bonfires set in barrels, which presaged heading changes that eventually brought the B-17 back over northern France. Ideally, its actual destination and drop location were obscured by all the maneuvering, like a bee sampling flowers in a garden the size of France. The cargo aboard Bowman's bomber was Sten guns, their stocks folded to fit in aluminum cans. For the ultimate Bastille Day flourish, the guns were attached to small colored parachutes, some red, some white, and others blue, Bowman remembered.[5]

The dark night only exaggerated the dangers of treetops and terrain as Bowman rode in the ball beneath his Fortress. Just ahead in the bomb bay, a plywoodlike material called button board held the cans of Sten guns. When the final bonfire was sighted and the bomb bay doors were open, it was up to the radio operator and the flight engineer to pull ropes that allowed the button board and its parachute cargo to spill out. For Dick Bowman, that nocturnal circuit over France rivaled a mission 2 days earlier to Munich as his longest, at 10 hours.

Bowman and the bomber crews had an unwanted kind of job security whenever they went to Merseberg to take out a coal oil jet fuel plant. "We'd blow the place up and they'd put it back together again in short order and we'd have to go back again." His log of 36 missions includes four trips to Merseberg.

Takeoffs and landings were often made in abysmal weather, he remembered. On the return flight, each Fortress group had the assigned radio frequency of a "buncher beacon" to guide them to their home field. Approaching the beacon, the B-17s would funnel in trail down to a landing. "It got hairy," Bowman remembered, because overcast sometimes obscured the next aircraft in the formation funneling down to land, and occasionally stray American and British aircraft wandered into the pattern as hundreds of B-17s were trying to recover after rigorous combat over the Continent.

The 96th Bomb Group operated *Five Grand,* the 5000th B-17 built by Boeing in Seattle. An oddity ever since Boeing workers painted their names all over its aluminum hide, the curiously marked *Five Grand* had been the subject of many publicity photos and stories. During its tenure in the 96th, the autographed bomber sustained damage in a belly landing, from which it was repaired and sent back into combat. Dick Bowman served as ball turret gunner on the repaired *Five Grand* for a couple of his missions, even adding his name to the turret's surface. But his pilot didn't much care for how the repaired *Five Grand* flew, Bowman remembered.

During Operation Market Garden, when Allied forces tried to secure bridges at Arnhem, Dick logged another departure in darkness from England, as 13 B-17s from the 96th Bomb Group bombed flak guns at daybreak in anticipation of the airborne assault to follow. As the morning sun began to color the eastern horizon, the Fortresses trundled home. Bowman, in his turret, watched the shift change in the skies as the Market Garden C-47s, some towing multiple gliders, passed in the opposite direction.

Dick Bowman filled in for the ball turret gunner of another crew once, putting him one mission ahead of the rest of his crew toward completing his tour of duty. They ultimately sustained injuries in a forced landing in Belgium, and he returned to the States by ship. "The boat was lousy," he recalled; men disembarked in New York with a variety of fleas and infestations, he said. Once home, Bowman became a gunnery instructor back where it all began for him at Tyndall. It was a well-deserved and appropriate opportunity to serve new gunners in the balmy Florida Gulf Coast.[6]

Jerome Cole, Combat Photographer

Words like "feisty" and "plucky" approach describing Jerry Cole, but they don't do him justice. A savvy photographer, New Yorker Jerome Cole was an enlisted photographic technician assigned to the brand-new 390th Bomb Group when it was still coalescing at Geiger Field west of Spokane, Washington, in 1943. Fresh out of photographic school at Lowry Field, Colorado, Cole's first airplane ride was in a light liaison plane orbiting low over the Geiger flight line as he hefted a K-20 aerial camera to record the 390th's receipt of brand-new B-17Fs.

When the 390th deployed to Framlingham, England, later that year, Cole was part of the contingent making

Jerry Cole worked nights readying 390th Bomb Group B-17 strike cameras for the next day's mission. K-21 cameras were mounted in some of the group's aircraft in a camera well beneath the radio room floor. *(Jerry Cole collection.)*

Jerry Cole promoted the best vantage point for dramatic wartime photography when he qualified as a 390th Bomb Group ball turret gunner so that he could ride in the turret carrying a hand-held K-24 camera with him. *(Cole collection.)*

a seagoing voyage to get there. Jerry's introduction to the war came the day after his arrival in the United Kingdom as he watched a returning formation of B-17s. One of the bombers stood out as it seemed to falter in flight before plunging abruptly earthward in a crash that instantly killed all aboard.[7]

In the United Kingdom, Jerry's duties typically involved configuring several 390th B-17s for strike photography the night before a mission. When the bombers returned from the mission, Jerry went from plane to plane retrieving cameras, sometimes amid piles of spent shell casings and bloody reminders of combat as he helped remove casualties from the Fortresses. Cameras were mounted beneath the floor of the radio room, where two small doors in the fuselage opened to expose the lenses to the target. The 390th quickly learned the camera hatch doors were not up to prolonged buffeting, and Jerry and his fellow camera technicians were instructed to pull the piano hinge wires from the doors, leaving a hole in the belly of the B-17s where the cameras unemotionally recorded the results of bombing missions.

To 18-year-old Jerry Cole, the strategic air war over Europe was an incredible, albeit sobering, adventure. Jerry looked for ways to get into the action. His avenue came when photographers assigned to provide combat aerial photos were transferred to another bomb group. Jerry further enhanced his usefulness by approaching the base gunnery school about taking the ball turret course. It was an off period for the school, so the otherwise idle instructors gave him a personalized course on the Sperry lower ball turret. This skill meant that Jerry could man the ball turret on portions of combat missions when photography was desired. He no longer had to rely only on taking pictures out the waist windows.

Cole and his compatriots were adept at jury-rigging equipment to get the job done, and he fitted an electrically driven K-24 camera and himself inside the ball turret so that he could deflect the turret to point down beneath the B-17, enabling him to photograph bombing results from his rotating perch. The ball turret was like having his own personal airplane in the formation, Jerry recalled, because it gave him the freedom to swing through 360 degrees in azimuth and 180 degrees in elevation beneath the big Fortress, where he could train his camera on other airplanes in the sky as well as on the ground below. When he flew on a bombing mission, Jerry typically replaced the regular ball turret gunner during the bomb run; at other times on the way to and from the target, Cole might man a waist gun, with the regular ball gunner back in his capsule.

During his first combat sortie in 1943, Jerry watched as escorting P-47 Thunderbolt fighters spewed bright white contrails overhead. The professional photographer in him prompted Cole to attach a red filter on the camera to increase the contrast between the contrails and the sky. He exposed an image of camouflaged B-17Fs and Thunderbolts weaving vapor tendrils over the Continent and went on with the mission. A minor light leak—common with many of the aerial cameras—slightly marred the negative once it was developed back at base, and Cole figured that the blemish diminished the usefulness of his photo. Little did he realize that airbrushed, cropped, and copied renditions of that photo would appear in books and periodicals for decades to follow, becoming an icon of the strategic air war over Europe.

On one sortie, Jerry entered a cramped ball turret that suffered from "creep," a mechanical malady that caused the turret to turn slowly in azimuth even when no input was made

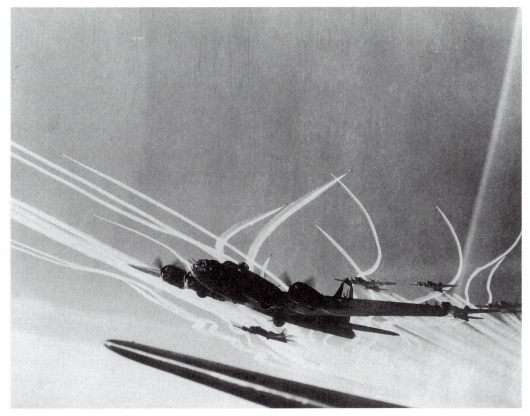

Lyrical yet deadly, this view of 390th Bomb Group B-17Fs and weaving P-47 escorts has been used in magazines and books ever since it was taken in 1943. By his recollection, photographer Jerome Cole said he took the photo and then virtually discarded it because of the light leak streaking the far right of the image. Though authorship of the photo was questioned by some members of the group later, Cole had some good evidence to support his claim. Regardless of the exact origin or precise date of the picture, it represents the B-17s of the 390th Bomb Group at war and stands as a tribute to the courage of all who served. *(Courtesy Jerome "Jerry" Cole.)*

Crewmen piled flak vests and aprons beside their B-17 after a mission. *(Brown/USAFA)*

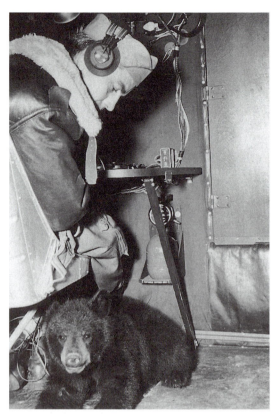

The 569th Bomb Squadron of the 390th Bomb Group took its bear cub mascot across the Atlantic to England in a B-17. *(Jerry Cole collection)*

to cause the rotation. Tiring of the slow spinning beneath the B-17, Jerry switched off the turret's hydraulic system to stop the uncommanded motion. After switching on and off a few times, the turret at last refused to power up, leaving Jerry suspended, with the turret pointing at an elevation that precluded his return inside the waist of the B-17. Cole had no choice but to ride the low-slung ball turret all the way home; even the emergency hand crank would not budge the sphere. If visions of making a disastrous belly landing occurred to the young photographer, he did not dwell on them. Back over Framlingham, the landing gear of the Fortress eased out of the nacelles without a hitch, and Jerry Cole, by necessity, saw the runway loom large from an exciting perch that was usually off limits during take-offs and landings.[8]

Cole's night shift enabled him to witness events the regular bomber crews missed. With radar-equipped Pathfinder B-17s shared by several bomb groups, the Pathfinder aircraft and crew assigned to a particular 390th mission typically arrived at Framlingham the night before. On one such staging mission to the 390th's airfield, members of the Pathfinder crew napped in the waist of their special Fortress during the ride. When the B-17 blew a tire on landing, the groggy crewmen aft of the flight deck awoke in the night and interpreted the jarring as an airborne emergency, Jerry recalled. The men leaped from the Fortress's exit, pulled ripcords, and immediately tumbled onto the ground. There was no way they could hide their misadventure, with billowing parachute canopies draped near the runway; at least their training had honed their responses to an automatic reaction. Later in the war, a Pathfinder arriving over Framlingham was less fortunate, as a lone marauding German fighter poured cannon fire into the solo nocturnal Fortress, causing it to crash to earth, plowing through a brick wall as it scattered parts over the countryside in a mortal slide.[9]

On one mission, Cole was surprised to see an extra large pile of flak vests—more than enough for the men on board—in the waist of the B-17 he entered. The reason only manifested itself later when, in the absence of enemy fighters, one of the gunners nested himself in this foxhole in the sky, sandwiching himself against perceived disaster, Jerry explained.

Not all of the risks to the men at Framlingham came from the Germans. While still in the United States, the 390th's 569th Bomb Squadron received a small black bear cub as a mascot, presented by a Native American group, Jerry explained. The cub rode in a B-17F all the way to England. Once on British soil, the growing bear was placed at the end of a length of chain near the base flagpole. Over time, the bear took to lunging at passersby, swiping the air with its claw-tipped paws when it reached the end of its chain, Cole said. Eventually, the bear was taken away, to a zoo, Jerry believed.[10]

Roy Test, Copilot

Perpetually wiry Roy Test sometimes wore his World War II "pinks and greens" uniform when he assisted at B-17 exhibits more than a half-century after the war. As he explained his experiences in B-17s, there was a quiet sense of urgency in his manner as he went about making sure the incredible human drama of the Eighth Air Force at war was not lost on younger generations.

Roy did not grow up around airplanes, although he worked a stint at building B-25s at North American Aviation in Inglewood, California, before joining the Army Air Forces. He nonetheless figured that flying would be for him. It had seemed so inaccessible, and now the wartime AAF might make it a reality. Not yet a college graduate, Roy saw his chance to become an Air Force officer. "After the war started, they relaxed the requirement" for college graduates, Test recounted. If he could pass a day-long grind of examinations, he could

Copilot Roy Test shrugged off snow flurries while standing in the back row, far right, for a portrait with his crew and three mechanics at Rapid City, South Dakota. *(Roy Test collection.)*

still make it into flight training. "I went to the library and I boned up," he explained. He passed and, in February 1943, traveled by train to a combination boot camp and ground school at what is now Lackland Air Force Base in San Antonio, Texas. After 3 months, "I was sent to Pine Bluff, Arkansas, for actual flying training," Roy related. That is where he soloed an open-cockpit monoplane Fairchild PT-19 trainer, surviving the scrutiny of a flight instructor who seemed bent on washing out students. The liberating solo flight released Test to practice in the air and then move on to Coffeyville, Kansas, to master the more complex Vultee BT-13 in 9 weeks of basic training.[11]

The durable B-25 twin-engine bombers had made a favorable impression on Roy when he worked at building them, so he asked for twin-engine advanced training after BT-13s and was sent to fly fabric-covered Cessna UC-78s at Altus, Oklahoma. After 9 weeks of mastering multiple throttles, Roy Test graduated as a rated second lieutenant. By Christmas of 1943, he was in a distribution center in Salt Lake City, Utah, before receiving orders to travel by troop train to Rapid City, South Dakota, where the 398th Bomb Group had just switched from being a replacement training unit to becoming a combat group destined for overseas migration. A world at war would dazzle Roy with images later, but for now, it was the little quirks that stayed in his mind: With bunks placed across the width of the troop cars, every stop and start on the way to Rapid City felt like it would spill him out, Test remembered.[12]

He was tapped to fly right seat as a new copilot in the 398th group. "We trained as a crew; we trained as a group." Roy and his crewmates got their hopes up while still at Rapid City when "each crew got a nice new bare-metal B-17G. . . . It was sort of a late Christmas present." The shiny new bombers inspired pride among the aircrews, some of whom shellacked wooden parts in their Fortresses, like the table top in the radio room, he remembered. Once the group finished its training, "We started leaving in April '44," Test said. More than a year of his life had been invested in flight training to make Roy capable to crew a four-engine B-17 over Germany in combat.

The group departed about a dozen bombers at a time. When Roy's formation left town, they buzzed a hotel about 10 or 12 stories high. "I could look straight out and see the hotel. I imagine that created quite a stir." It was like the stir a pistol-firing posse might have made galloping out of Dodge City in the previous century; like the stir knights, planted on armored horses, might have had hundreds of years before, streamers waving, as they rode forth on a Crusade.

At Grand Island, Nebraska, Roy and his crewmates were issued .45-caliber automatic pistols and told to post a 24-hour guard on their new B-17, which was fitted with the secret Norden bombsight by that time. Outfitted for the Atlantic ferry flight, Roy's next stop was Bangor, Maine, followed by Goose Bay, Labrador, and after a delay to fix a recalcitrant IFF (Identification, Friend or Foe) unit, it was on to Iceland. Upon reaching the 398th's assigned base in England at Nuthampstead, Roy and crew turned in "their" B-17G, which needed to be fitted with minor modifications such as a chaff port in the radio room. "We were assigned another late model bare-skinned B-17G that we called the *Bad Penny*," Test remembered. "It never did get any nose art (or nickname lettering)," he added.[13]

Roy said the whole crew decided to fly as many missions as quickly as possible to rack up their combat tour in a short period of time. Summer meant the best flying weather. "I would hate to have been over there in bad weather," Roy explained. At that point, the 398th Bomb Group used nine-man crews instead of ten, taking along only one waist gunner, Roy said. "We didn't really need 10 men," he explained. And a check of 398th fighter claims seems to bear this out, as the 398th Bomb Group only tallied five enemy aircraft shot down, two damaged, and 11 probables.[14]

After a few shakedown practice missions over England, Roy Test took up his position in the right-hand seat for the crew's first combat sortie, a 20 May 1944 venture over Villacoublay, near Paris. By 24 May, Roy Test was passing over Berlin. "On that mission to Berlin, we had fighters come in at us head-on." His crew kept up the tempo and received credit for 32 missions in 77 days. Through it all, Test recalled, his crew did not have the opportunity to fire on any German fighters, and nobody on the crew was injured. But flak was ever-present. "I think nearly every mission we picked up flak holes in the plane," he said.[15]

Once, right after bombs away, Roy made an emergency shutdown of one engine when an oil gauge showed low pressure. The B-17 dropped out of formation as Test and his pilot discussed options. Making an educated guess that the problem may have been the oil gauge and not the engine, they restarted the powerplant after trying for about 5 minutes and were pleased to find it performing well. There was a corollary to the many tales of lone B-17 stragglers limping across the Continent, trying to reach England before German fighters could get to them. On this day, Roy Test's B-17 located about 10 or 15 stragglers, and all formed their own grouping for mutual protection, flying an impromptu formation back across the English Channel, where the various bombers peeled off to reach their diverse assigned airfields. Test recalled the formation was "rather irregular . . . but we felt better."[16]

Roy Test's pilot had no desire to hog the flying. "He was happy to have some relief," Roy explained. Over Europe, Roy and the pilot traded formation-flying chores every 15 or 20 minutes, sometimes more frequently. The work was exhausting, at altitude on oxygen, trying to keep a heavy bomber on course, and altitude, and in proximity to others as they all bobbled in air currents and prop wash. The exertion in the cockpit burned calories, and Roy said he sometimes didn't even need to plug in his electrically heated flying suit to stay warm, even as other members of the crew were grateful for the artificial heat.[17]

One tenet of strategic bombing became evident to Roy Test during his tour: Radar bombing was only accomplished against targets in Germany out of concern for possible collateral damage to civilians in occupied countries, he said. Roy's last mission came on 4 August 1944, a summertime sortie to the secret German research facility at Peenemunde. "We knew that was where the rocket scientists were working," Roy commented. Those scientists and their facilities were fiercely protected by thick antiaircraft fire, he recalled. "Berlin, Peenemunde, and Hamburg were always a lot of flak . . . That was really our only enemy," he said. "That's the nice thing about having your own fighters in the air."[18]

While Roy Test and his fellow crewmembers were racing to complete their required combat missions, the number of missions comprising a combat tour went up from 25 to 30 and then again to 35. Since Eighth Air Force kept raising the requirement in the middle of Test's tour, his crew was given credit for three missions in a formula that ultimately let them rotate home after flying 32 missions. Roy readily acknowledged the increased dangers his predecessors in B-17s had faced the year before he arrived in Europe: "It was much easier to get 35 missions in '44 than it was to get 25 missions in '43," he noted.[19]

Roy Test said he was apprehensive before his first, and subsequent, combat missions. But he faced it with a matter-of-fact stoicism. "The fact was we had to do it. That's what we were there for." He said his crew felt, "We gotta win this damn war, and the sooner the better."

Asked if he would like to fly a B-17 again this many years after the war, his response was crisp: "I'd love to. And I'd want to sit in the right seat. I feel the most comfortable there."[20]

Notes

1. Interview, Frederick A. Johnsen with Richard E. Bowman, 8 May 1999.
2. *Ibid.*
3. *Ibid.*
4. *Ibid.*
5. *Ibid.*
6. *Ibid.*
7. Conversation, Frederick A. Johnsen with Jerome Cole, 7 February 1999.

8. *Ibid.*
9. *Ibid.*
10. *Ibid.*
11. Interview, Frederick A. Johnsen with Roy Test, 8 May 1999.
12. *Ibid.*
13. *Ibid.*
14. Interview, Frederick A. Johnsen with Roy Test, 8 May 1999, and Roger A. Freeman, *The Mighty Eighth—A History of the U.S. 8th Army Air Force,* Doubleday, Garden City, N.Y., 1970.
15. Interview, Frederick A. Johnsen with Roy Test, 8 May 1999.
16. *Ibid.*
17. *Ibid.*
18. *Ibid.*
19. *Ibid.*
20. *Ibid.*

CHAPTER
5

By Example

Arming the Flying Fortress

Although prewar B-17 armaments were minimized because of the euphoric pronouncements of bomber advocates about fighter inadequacies, the number of machine guns carried aloft still inspired the most unforgettable moniker of all military aircraft: Flying Fortress. All gun emplacements on the original Model 299, as well as B-17s through the D-model, were hand-held flexible mounts strong-armed by the gunners without benefit of hydraulics or electric motors. The Sperry and Bendix companies devised American power turrets to increase the defensive shield around B-17s starting with the bigger tailed B-17E.

Marksmen

If prewar bombers were supposed to outrun ineffectual fighters and if a sprinkling of flexible gun mounts were to be sufficient for any intruders, this misperception, coupled with stingy peacetime budget considerations, left the early training of Flying Fortress gunners largely to chance. Gen. Curtis LeMay, who entered combat as commander of the B-17-equipped 305th Bomb Group, later described early combat gunnery as "horrible." "Gunnery was pretty low on the totem pole in peacetime," LeMay recalled. "You never could get enough ammunition."

   To his dismay, when he was shaping up the fledgling 305th Bomb Group in the Mojave Desert before leading it overseas for combat, LeMay learned that some of the gunners assigned to his B-17s had never even flown in an airplane. Their previous training consisted of firing truck-mounted guns. LeMay explained: "I got my gunners one ride in an airplane, shooting at the desert as you ran across at low altitude. That was it; then we went into combat." Then-Colonel LeMay joined others in Eighth Air Force in 1942 clamoring for better gunners produced with better training back home.[1]

Before the Ball

In the prewar effort to improve the Fortress's defensive capabilities, Sperry devised a remotely operated lower turret for the B-17E to complement the manned Sperry upper tur-

117

Early Fortresses like the Model 299 prototype used a hand-operated spherical gun mount, photographed with a single .50-caliber machine gun on 24 July 1935. Bombardier's sighting window was located farther aft under the nose. *(Boeing via SDAM.)*

ret also introduced on the E-model. Designated Sperry 645705D, the pillbox-shaped remote turret mounted two .50-caliber machine guns in a ventral location just aft of the radio compartment. Inside the waist of the B-17E aft of the turret, a remote sighting station on the floor accommodated a prone gunner who faced aft. As he manipulated the computing gunsight in its cradle, it moved in azimuth and elevation, transferring those movements to the turret as well. The gunsight was housed in a shallow Plexiglas dome protruding beneath the fuselage. Scanning windows similar to those applied to B-24 lower waist areas were devised in an effort to help the lower turret gunner see his attackers. A column from the top of the fuselage attached to the turret.[2]

The design of the Sperry remote ventral turret was cumbersome to some users and was said to promote disorientation in a few gunners. Fortunately, Sperry designed a much more workable manned ball turret successor to the short-lived remote ventral turret, and it was introduced on later B-17Es and continued, with some modification, to be the lower hemisphere defense for subsequent B-17s and B-24s as well. During

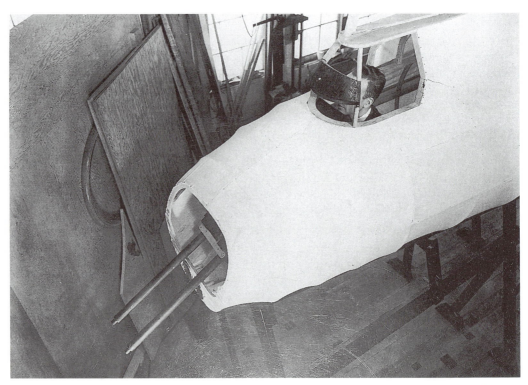

On 13 July 1940, a fabric-covered mockup of the manned tail gun emplacement introduced on the B-17E was photographed in the Boeing plant. Tail guns proved as significant as nose guns for protecting bombers because fighters had an easier shot when attacking from the front or the rear than from the sides, where deflection made computation of the aim point more complex. *(Boeing via SDAM.)*

production of B-17Es in Seattle, aircraft numbers 41-2393 through 41-2504 had provisions to alternately mount the ball turret or the remote ventral turret; E-models 41-2505 through 41-2669 and 41-9011 through 41-9245, the last of the B-17Es, used only the manned ball turret.[3]

Sperry Lower Ball Turret

The wartime *Gunner's Information File* praised the Sperry manned ball turret:

> The Sperry Lower Ball, mounted in the belly of the B-17, is a deadly and efficient defender of the bomber's once soft underside. Its guns sweep in a full circle and offer protection from any fighter who dips below the bomber's level; its sight, the Sperry K-4, computes deflections automatically even when the gunner, swinging around below the plane, is unable to tell exactly which way he is facing.[4]

An electric motor kept hydraulic pressure applied to the Sperry ball turret to provide its power for elevation and azimuth. Gunners were instructed to stow the turret with guns at 0 degrees elevation and trailing straight back toward the tail. The heavy ball turret was finely balanced. The gunner had to ensure that it was locked in place before he tried to enter or exit, or else "it may

A fabric boot closed off the aft fuselage while allowing flexible movement for the two .50-caliber machine guns installed in B-17s beginning with the B-17E, as photographed 1 October 1941. Angled blast tubes were sometimes bolted to gun muzzles. Gunner relied on small ring-and-bead gunsight outside his window that was cabled to move with the travel of the guns. *(Boeing photo.)*

Many World War II AAF bomber gunners learned about moving targets by firing shotguns at thrown skeet while riding in the back of a truck. A group of students at Las Vegas, Nevada, was photographed ready to get underway on 21 April 1943. *(AAF.)*

In August 1943, B-17 number 23302 (a Douglas-built F-model) took hits to its windscreen, panes of which were held up for a damage assessment photo later. Typical B-17 windscreens were safety glass sandwiches with an air space between inner and outer layers. Later, thick bullet resistant armor windscreens were developed. *(Jerry Cole collection.)*

Airmen mugged with a jacketless actor-turned-captain Clark Gable in England in 1943, where Gable made a documentary film, *Combat America,* about gunners. *(AAF via Bowman collection.)*

swivel and break a man's leg or snap him almost in two as he attempts to enter," the Gunner's Information File explained. The gunner also was instructed to vacate the turret before landing and to stay outside during all ground operations: "The ball turret, hanging down beneath the plane, is no place to be when the bomber is moving along the ground."[5]

To enter the turret, the gunner pointed the guns straight down, which placed the entry hatch up, inside the fuselage, and clear of the floor. (Some photos of stricken Fortresses in combat reveal ball turret guns deflected down, suggesting the gunner had moved it to that position to evacuate it.)

Dropping the Ball

Unlike the B-24 Liberator, whose lower ball turret retracted inside the fuselage when not in use, the ball turret beneath the B-17 was permanently suspended because the B-17's tailwheel stance allowed sufficient ground clearance for the lower turret. While this simplified the mechanics of ball turret installations in Fortresses, it posed a problem during belly landings, when the Sperry ball turret got forced up into the fuselage, sometimes breaking the back of an otherwise reparable Fortress. Eighth Air Force crews, if they had time to contemplate a belly landing, took to jettisoning ball turrets to minimize damage to the fuselage.

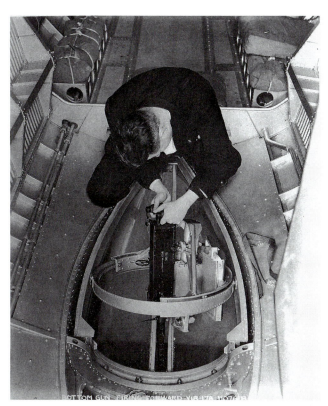

Awkward ventral blister gun survived through production of prewar B-17Bs. Its efficacy was a far cry from the ultimate manned Sperry lower ball turret. *(Boeing photo.)*

Early B-17Es warmed up on a misty morning, their remotely sighted Sperry pillbox lower turrets and aft-mounted sighting stations visible beneath the fuselages aft of the bomb bays. *(SDAM.)*

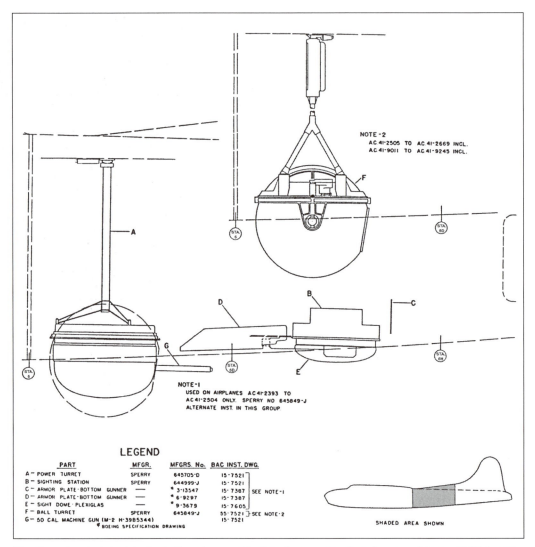

Phantom drawing depicted relative placement of early unmanned and manned lower B-17 turrets, plus Plexiglas sighting bubble (part E) for the unmanned version. (*AAF B-17 erection and mainte-nance manual via Don Keller.*)

For the benefit of aircrews, Boeing analyzed a pair of B-17G belly landings which had different consequences: "In the first landing the ball turret was jettisoned. The airplane was landed in a level attitude with both the main wheels and tail wheel retracted. The chin turret dome was dented, and some damage was caused by the radio compass loop antenna rolling back underneath the body. Except for abrasions the airplane structure was otherwise intact." On the second B-17G, the plane landed with the ball turret still in place. The aircraft was settled in a tail down attitude this time. "Upon impact the tail gun enclosure was knocked off, and both the chin turret and ball turret were driven up into the body causing considerable damage." This B-17 was salvaged.[6]

Boeing advised leaving the ball turret yoke intact and unbolting only the turret sphere. "Only two tools, a Crescent wrench and a hammer, are required to do the job. Two men can do it in about 20 minutes." After removing the turret's azimuth gear case, disabling four safety retaining hooks with a hammer or socket wrench, the 12 nuts retaining the turret to its yoke were removed. Boeing's instructions noted: "The turret may momentarily hang up on the fire cut-off cam, but a swift kick on the aft side of the ball will dislodge it." As Emerson became the contractor building ball turrets, replacing Briggs who had contracted to produce the units earlier, a new-style yoke was introduced, but the jettisoning procedure remained the same.[7]

Sperry Upper Turret

Behind the cockpit of B-17s beginning with the E-model, a Sperry top turret mounted a pair of .50-caliber M-2 machine guns. Like the Sperry-designed lower ball turret, the Sperry upper turret was hydraulically activated. The turret had a full 360-degree sweep in azimuth and could elevate from 5 degrees below horizontal to 85 degrees overhead. Versions of the Sperry upper turret used six ammunition cans, three for each gun. Each can carried about 125 rounds. A canvas bag caught

Early-style B-17 ball turret used streamlined side panels that made the turret more of a true sphere and covered the trunnion mounts. Later production did away with these Plexiglas and aluminum fairings, exposing the trunnions. *(Jerry Cole.)*

shells and links from the guns. The turret's computing sight lent itself to an inverted version for the lower ball turret. The B-17 upper turret's dome metamorphosed over the span of Fortress production, with diminishing metal webs between glazing panels providing an ever-better field of view for the gunner.[8]

By the time Seattle war workers painted their names all over the 5,000th Boeing-built B-17 in 1944, the ball turret no longer carried streamlined side fairings. In the photo, the ball turret and chin turret for the 5,000th Seattle Fortress, nicknamed *Five Grand,* awaited installation. *(Boeing.)*

Sighting a ball turret on the night shift, Boeing workers completed their task in the rain as smoke and tracers spat from the two .50-caliber weapons. *(Bowman collection.)*

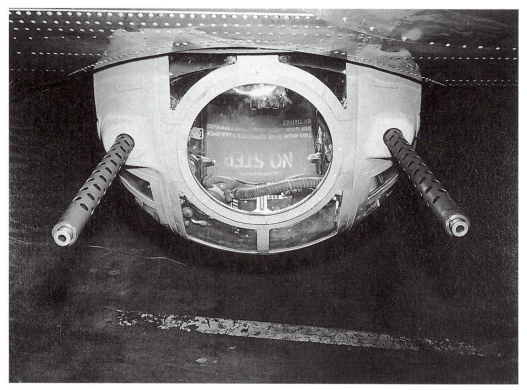

Circular ball turret gunner's window offered an incredible view of the war raging around a Flying Fortress. Encapsulated gunner moved with the turret. *(Boeing via Bowman.)*

The view inside a B-17F ball turret shows black box of Sperry computing gunsight. Stirrup handles on either side of circular window were for charging each gun. Scalloped seat was made of armor plate; some had a heating fixture attached. *(Boeing via Bowman.)*

Nose Guns for the F-Model

B-17Fs initially used sockets for ineffectual .30-caliber hand-held machine guns in the upper front portion of the nose Plexiglas. Soon, a .50-caliber cheek gun appeared in a flush window on either side of the nose, and the .30 went away. As soon as German fighters learned the advisability of making hurtling headlong attacks at B-17 formations, the inadequacy of these armaments was manifest.

Variations to B-17F frontal armament included the institution of the .50-caliber cheek guns beginning on B-17F-55-BO products built in Seattle. Then, with the last 70 B-17F-85-BO variants, nose armament was raised to three .50-calibers, including a center-mounted flexible weapon. The center nose gun was supported by an internal welded tube truss, while the early flush cheek guns were carried in steel K-4 eyeball sockets supported by steel stands on the window sills. Later, some B-17Fs received forward-protruding cheek windows that used cylindrical K-5 gun mounts.

On the Douglas production line, B-17F-1-DL variants left the factory woefully undergunned with a single .30 in the nose in addition to the other turrets and gun emplacements elsewhere on the airframe. B-17F-10-DLs starting with number 42-2992 had two nose-mounted .50-calibers, which were raised to three guns in the nose starting with B-17F-35-DL number 42-3210. Vega

Stout hanger made of tubing supported the ball turret in the waist of a B-17. If a belly landing was forecast, crews were urged to disconnect the ball turret from the hanger and let it fall free because it could cause serious damage to the bomber if left in place. *(Boeing via Bowman collection.)*

Addition of a forward-firing .50-caliber machine gun in the upper nose glazing of Eighth Air Force B-17Fs made the nose even more crowded than before. Rounded triangular bomb-aiming window was made of optical-quality glass layers with an air space between to promote defrosting. First Lt. A. L. Dentoni of the 385th Bomb Group can be seen peering around bagged bombsight. *(AAF photo.)*

F-models underwent similar iterations; the center-mounted nose gun was often a modification-center addition to keep from slowing the pace of production at the factory.[9]

The Bendix chin turret, which had proven itself to be the lone bright spot in the YB-40 bomber escort experiment, was adopted for regular Fortress production. Some aircraft ordered as late-production B-17Fs were built with chin turrets, although their nomenclature was changed to B-17G to reflect the magnitude of the change. There appears to have been initial optimism about the efficacy of new nose armaments, but it was later rethought. When the chin turret was introduced, G-models deleted the flexible cheek guns, only to reintroduce them later in G-series production. Boeing B-17Gs were produced without cheek guns at the factory until those flexible nose guns were reintroduced on the last 35 bombers of Block 60. Douglas B-17Gs brought back cheek guns with Block 25 deliveries. Vega G-models added cheek guns in bulged windows on Block 35 aircraft.

The K-5 gun mount in each cheek window frame occupied the lowest frontal cutout. Immediately above this was the small sighting window, which was hinged to swing inward for cleaning. The top frontal cheek window was designated a scanning window. The large formed Plexiglas side window in the cheek installation was a "pickup window" for target acquisition.[10]

On camouflaged B-17Gs, the rapid fading of the original olive drab paint provides a telltale clue to the post-production modification with cheek guns that often took place. Darkened paint around cheek windows on early B-17Gs indicates the latter-day installation of these guns in addition to the vaunted chin turret.

Taking It on the Chin

The Bendix A16 chin turret survived several false starts to become a potently functional armament for the B-17G. In the formative years of power turret development in the United States, Bendix Aviation Corporation produced an aluminum-shrouded pillbox-shaped turret initially used as a lower hemisphere armament on early B-24Ds and B-25s. The turret was not well liked as a lower gun emplacement. The gunner knelt in the fuselage over the turret and viewed the world through a periscopic gunsight. While the gunner and the sight's eyepiece remained stationary inside the bomber, the turret and the rest of the sight could rotate 360 degrees in azimuth. Disorientation was not uncommon, and most B-17 and B-24 armaments would rely on direct line-of-sight optics where the gunner moved with his guns.

The Bendix turret was mounted in the chin of a B-17F as ideas for the bomber escort Fortress were hatched. It was a fortuitous installation; in the spacious nose of a B-17, the gunner (bombardier) sat on a chair that had the best view of the war through the large Plexiglas enclosure. A swing-out arm culminating in grips for the chin turret could be brought to a comfortable position in front of the gunner. An electric gunsight hung from a bracket

Flush cheek gun mount on B-17Fs used K-4 eyeball socket. *(Jerry Cole.)*

Better forward field of fire was achieved with protruding cheek gun in heavy aluminum frame, with K-5 cylindrical gun mount, as used on *The Dull Tool.* Both F-models served with the 390th Bomb Group. *(Jerry Cole.)*

With all the metal flying around during attacks on B-17 formations, it's no surprise this 390th Bomb Group F-model took a hit in the Plexiglas nose. Center nose gun has been removed, showing details of the reinforced gun mount applied to many Eighth Air Force B-17Fs. *(Jerry Cole.)*

To maximize firepower, Eighth Air Force formations used stepped boxes of aircraft to allow many guns to bear on attacking fighters. *(Jerry Cole.)*

Bombardier William J. Hyde used gloved hands to grasp the grips of a cheek gun E-11 recoil adapter in the nose of his 388th Bomb Group B-17 on 2 July 1944. Ring and snap swivel on back of recoil adapter led to a cable to support and balance the gun. *(Brown/USAFA.)*

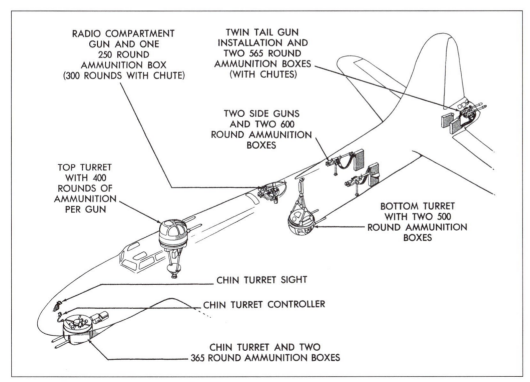

Armament drawing depicting early B-17G showed chin turret with no other frontal guns, side-by-side waist windows, ball turret, factory tail gun mount, and open-style ring-mounted radio room gun. Even with the addition of a power top turret beginning with the B-17E, radio room guns lingered and evolved well into G-model production. *(AAF B-17 erection and maintenance manual via Don Keller.)*

At Las Vegas Army Airfield in January 1944, First Lt. H. L. Walker devised a training device to allow chin turret gunners to practice on the Nevada ranges. As he would in a B-17G, the gunner student sat above the turret on the training truck, with turret grip control in front of him and moving gunsight overhead. *(AAF photo.)*

In England in October 1944, the 303d Bomb Group used an indoor trainer to teach gunners coordination when tracking projected targets. Chin turret gunsight was connected to movement of the turret, so the sight moved as well. *(AAF photo.)*

in the upper portion of the nose. The sight bracket was motorized; as the turret grips were turned to traverse or elevate the guns, the sight moved accordingly. The whole operation was much more natural and less confusing than the earlier belly-mounted Bendix units of B-24s and B-25s.

The two .50-caliber M-2 machine guns in the chin turret could be elevated 26 degrees above horizontal and depressed 46 degrees below the horizon. Lateral travel was 86 degrees in either direction off centerline. Curved ammunition cans were integral to the turret and held 365 rounds. The chin turret had two speed ranges of motion: Low speed allowed the turret to track anywhere from one-fourth of a degree of movement per second to 12 degrees per second, and a handle-mounted high-speed switch boosted the speed up through a range of 33 degrees per second. Actual speed of gun travel was dictated by the amount of displacement the gunner put on the grips.[11]

Early chin turret installations were made on Fortresses using the elongated F-style Plexiglas nosepiece designed without the chin turret in mind. During production of B-17Gs, at least two visible changes to the nose Plexiglas took place. Beginning with B-17G-BO number 42-31332, B-17G-DL 42-37943, and B-17G 42-39858, a new plastic nose design was introduced. A Boeing technical publication said that the new nose improved sighting characteristics for the chin turret and reduced "the effect of gun blast on the bombardier's window . . . The nose is now one-piece and five inches shorter than the one on the B-17F."[12]

Many chin turrets were installed with zippered canvas boots covering the machine gun elevation slots. As the guns moved up or down, a metal collar around each gun barrel simultaneously opened and closed the zippered wind baffle. Late in production, these canvas wind baffles were replaced with metal strips similar to those used on the top turret. This change was introduced on the production line beginning with B-17G-105-BO number 43-39169 and Vega B-17G-80-VE 44-8765. Not initially assigned to Douglas G-models, this change, like so many Fortress modifications, may show up in field changes on other B-17s.[13]

The Bendix A16 chin turret added more than 400 lb to the weight of a Flying Fortress.[14] If this imposed any performance penalty, it was nonetheless welcomed for the protection it afforded the B-17G. (In fact, the laden B-17G was slower than the E-model; the B-17G cruised at 182 mph compared with the E-model's cruise speed of 210, continuing a gradual performance decline that began with the F-model, as combat-worthy Fortresses packed on additional weight.)

Beginning with Seattle-built Block-90 G-model 43-38574 and Vega B-17G-75-VE 44-8601, the chin turret controller was fitted with an intercom thumb button; at the same time in production, a radio intercom foot switch was placed on the floor near the bombardier's right foot, providing another means of communication. "This change will provide a switch which may be operated without removing the hands from the guns or bombsight," a Boeing technical publication explained.[15]

B-17 waist windows also underwent changes during the life of the G-model. Initial B-17Gs were produced with the same drafty open-air waist window gun emplacements that had been introduced back on the prewar B-17E. But just as designers were finding ways to close

Waist gunners aboard a B-17E demonstrated use of their weapons with ammunition cans, later superseded by flexible ammunition chutes leading to large boxes. Close proximity of waist gunners led to staggering of waist windows during B-17G production. On open-style B-17 waist windows, the hatches moved forward on tracks to expose the gun. *(SDAM.)*

off the wind that blasted B-24 waist gunners, so too were their B-17 counterparts gaining the benefits of enclosed waist positions. Early enclosed B-17G waist emplacements used a heavily ribbed hatch divided with three Plexiglas windows and housing a spring-balanced K-5 gun mount. The gun mount was centered on the bottom of the window sill.

Cramped quarters in the narrowing waist of the B-17 prompted a redesign of waist gun location. The right waist window was moved forward more than one window opening span; this created an offset for the gunners inside to increase their maneuvering room in a running battle with fighters. The relocation of the right waist window forward caused the national star insignia to be moved aft of the window on the right side only.

Along with the staggering of the waist gun windows, the heavy metal ribbing and, eventually, the K-5 gun mount were replaced with a clear-view Plexiglas window curved to conform to the fuselage radius and cut out to allow use of a K-6 gun mount. The K-6 used a stamped iron "can" through which a gun mount protruded. The sheet-metal cylindrical can allowed the gun to be traversed in azimuth without breaking the loose wind seal between the can and the Plexiglas cutout. Inside the can, the gun mount could be elevated and depressed. Waist guns in K-6 mounts could use iron ring-and-bead gunsights or simple illuminated noncomputing reflector sights.

Staggered waist windows went into the production flow beginning with Seattle B-17G number 42-102374, Douglas B-17G number 42-37989, and Vega G-model 44-8101. Modification centers performed this rearrangement of waist guns on some previous G-models.[16]

The final upgrade to B-17G waist windows was the introduction of the K-7 gun mount, very similar in outward appearance to the slightly smaller K-6. The K-7 was designed as part of a gun system. It contained gears and cable fittings to send azimuth and elevation

Evidently an attempt to keep waist gunners from firing into parts of their own B-17 in the heat of battle, this right waist window has bent metal rods placed in a way that probably kept the gun from traversing past the wing and propellers in front (right) and the tail to the rear (left). *(AAF photo.)*

Add-on enclosure for left waist window of a 92d Bomb Group B-17 used heavy ribbing for window panels and a spring-balanced K-5 gun mount. *(AAF photo.)*

information to a K-13 gunsight, which was mounted on a special plate on an E-13 recoil adapter. The K-13 gunsight was a computing sight that used inputs to move the lighted reticle on the sight glass to correct for lead and windage. This made the gunner's chore easier in the heat of battle. Instead of trying to compute lead and windage mentally, the gunner armed with a K-13 sight simply placed the reticle on the target at all times.

During B-17G production in 1943, waist gun ammunition box size was increased from 250 rounds to 600 rounds per gun, belt-fed to each weapon. This change was instituted on B-17G-15-BO number 42-31332, B-17G-15-DL number 42-37804, and B-17G-5-VE number 42-39858.[17]

Prewar Fortresses going back to the prototype Model 299 had sometimes been fitted with radio room guns. The dorsal radio room hatch on aircraft including the F- and G-models was removable in flight, and during the production of B-17Fs, a single flexible .50-caliber machine gun was placed in this opening, mounted to a ring. Typically supplied with 300 rounds of ammunition, the radio gun installation lingered into B-17G production.

Along the way, at least two variations of enclosed radio room guns were used. A factory installation put a K-6 gun mount at an angle on the rear sill of the radio room hatch, with a cutout in the hatch's Plexiglas to accommodate the K-6, much as was done in enclosed waist windows. While this diminished draft and noise in the radio room, the installation also decreased the gun's field of travel. A Boeing technical bulletin described advantages to this arrangement: "This installation seals the [radio operator's] compartment against loss of heat and mounts the gun at the firing position. It need only be unstrapped and charged before going into action. The gun can be quickly jettisoned by pulling the [mounting] pins.

On Fortresses equipped with an open radio room gun, an ingenious ring mount with rollers allowed a T-shaped gun mount to traverse from side to side while the ring pivoted for elevation. *(Brown/USAFA.)*

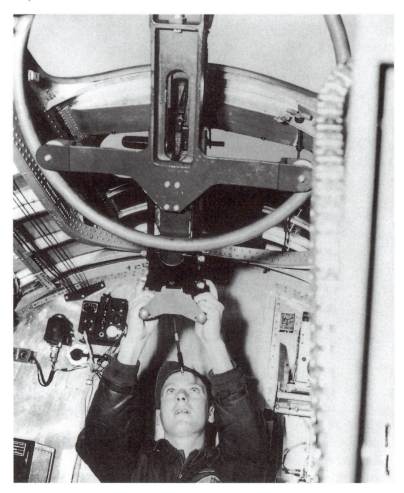

Ditching procedure is unchanged because the hatch is still quickly removable." Boeing introduced this change on the assembly line beginning with B-17G-85-BO number 43-38274. Concurrently, since the radio operator now would sight his gun through a closed Plexiglas window, a circular window clean-off door about 6 in in diameter was placed in the clear glazing of the dorsal hatch.[18]

Meanwhile, Eighth Air Force experimented with a heavy aluminum stamping into which a K-5 gun mount was bolted. This unit also was attached to the rear of the radio room hatch opening, and the hatch was truncated to fit. Still later in B-17G production at all three plants, the radio room gun was deleted entirely as combat experience dictated the most and least effective gun locations for the Flying Fortress.

During B-17G production, a decal was affixed near the radio room hatch instructing personnel in flight: "Before removing radio compartment hatch, raise wind deflector and open rear door in radio compartment."[19]

The lack of tail guns on B-17s built up through the D-model reflected 1930s thinking, when the early Fortresses could outrun many adversaries, and persistent fighter attacks from any quarter were to be met by flexible guns in the waist as well as other fuselage blisters. This thinking fell before fighter advances, and the B-17E placed a tail gunner behind the retracted tailwheel in a cupola fitted with a padded bicycle-type seat as well as kneepads. Armed with a pair of .50-caliber guns in E-11 recoil adapters hanging from a post, the

When the late-war Cheyenne tail turret was introduced during B-17G production, it used a metal "pumpkin" to cap the aft fuselage, with the guns elevating in slots, while the whole pumpkin traversed from side to side. In the photo, an armorer reached into the spent shell ejection chute. *(AAF photo.)*

B-17 tail gunner effectively diminished the likelihood of a successful attack from the rear. But the mount, which remained essentially the same from the B-17E throughout F-model production and well into G-series Fortresses, had some limitations.

Boeing went to work on a new design, a rounded tail mount sometimes called the "pumpkin" because of its shape and technically known as the Cheyenne installation because many were added to new G-models at the United Airlines Fortress modification center in Cheyenne, Wyoming. A papier-mâché mockup of the Cheyenne tail section, the inspiration for which came when a Boeing mockup maker saw a lightweight dress mannequin of the same materials, was made in Seattle to check the fit of the new design. To keep aircraft production lines moving without interruption, some improved features like the Cheyenne tail emplacement were initially added at postproduction modification centers while the factories geared up to introduce the changes on the assembly floor with the least amount of disruption.

Benefits of the Cheyenne tail gun emplacement were more room, a vastly increased cone of fire for the tail guns, and a larger curved Plexiglas window for the gunner. Where the older tail gun emplacement had relied on a slab of bullet resistant glass facing aft, the Cheyenne unit had the armor glass attached to the gun hanging post inside the curved window. In this way, wherever the gunner moved the guns, the armor glass was placed between him and his target, who was presumably shooting at him.

As with other armament upgrades on B-17Gs, Cheyenne tail sections were both a production item and an aftermarket piece depending on when the aircraft was manufactured.

Some photos of Eighth Air Force formations reveal older camouflaged B-17Gs sporting bright silver aluminum Cheyenne tail gun emplacements added in the field. An AAF armament tally says that the Cheyenne mount was used on Boeing-built G-models starting with aircraft number 43-38473, the last B-17G-85-BO; on Douglas-built Fortresses, the Cheyenne was used beginning with number 44-6251, the first B-17G-50-DL; on Vega B-17s, the Cheyenne tail was used starting with aircraft number 44-8287, a B-17G-55-VE.[20]

Notes

1. *Strategic Air Warfare,* USAF Warrior Studies, Office of Air Force History, Washington, D.C., 1988.
2. Excerpts from T.O. 01-20EE-2 B-17E *Erection and Maintenance Manual.*
3. *Ibid.*
4. "The Sperry Upper," AAF *Gunner's Information File,* May 1944.
5. *Ibid.*
6. "Removal of the Ball Turret in Flight," *Boeing Field Service News,* issue not noted.
7. *Ibid.*
8. "The Sperry Ball," AAF *Gunner's Information File,* May 1944
9. "Monthly Chart—Armament and Bomb Installations—AAF Aircraft," Chief, Engineering Division, Air Technical Service Command, Wright Field, Oh., 1 August 1945.
10. "Cheek Guns Installed. BDV 822," *Boeing Field Service News,* Issue No. 32, 8 May 1944.
11. *Operation and Service Manual for the Electric Power Operated Bendix Chin Turret,* Bendix Products Division, Bendix Aviation Corporation, South Bend, Ind., 15 May 1943.
12. "Plexiglas Nose Revised. BDV 725," *Boeing Field Service News,* Issue No. 18, 25 October 1943.
13. "Chin Turret Metal Gun Enclosures. BDV 716-13," *Boeing Field Service News,* Issue No. 51, 29 January 1945.
14. *Index of Army-Navy Aeronautical Equipment—Armament,* Technical Order No. 11-1-64, published by authority of the Commanding General, Army Air Forces, 10 June 1944.
15. "Microphone Switches. BDV 923-P1," and "Step-On Microphone Switch. BDV 923-1," *Boeing Field Service News,* Issue No. 40, 28 August 1944.
16. "Enclosed Waist Guns Installed. BDV 517," *Boeing Field Service News,* Issue No. 29, 27 March 1944.
17. "600 Round Ammunition Boxes. BDV 790," *Boeing Field Service News,* Issue No. 18, 25 October 1943.
18. "Enclosed Radio Operator's Gun. BDV 823A," *Boeing Field Service News,* Issue No. 38, 31 July 1944.
19. "Instructions for Removing Escape Hatch. BDV 675-7," *Boeing Field Service News,* issue not noted.
20. "Monthly Chart—Armament and Bomb Installations—AAF Aircraft," Chief, Engineering Division, Air Technical Service Command, Wright Field, Oh., 1 August 1945.

Other Lands

Foreign Countries Also Flew the Fortress

Great Britain clamored for American warplanes before the United States entered the war. The U.S. Army Air Corps threaded its path through divergent issues on this topic. Foreign military sales might be the only economic boost available to push American aircraft manufacturers into the physical plant expansion the Air Corps wanted to see, and yet any diversion of American production output competed with the Air Corps' own expansion plans.

In the case of Boeing, the British quest for airpower showed up in a licensing agreement by which Boeing built DB-7B versions of the Douglas A-20 Havoc attack bomber initially for France (assumed by England when France fell), even as the Air Corps made ready to turn over 20 secondhand B-17Cs to England. Much as the Air Corps let England get some of the first production B-24 Liberators, the diversion of older C-model Fortresses to Great Britain in effect allowed the Air Corps to modernize its own fleet with later production. The Boeing assembly line for DB-7Bs helped the company pay for plant expansion that the Air Corps would ultimately use for mass production of B-17s.

The British continued to receive small numbers of B-17Es and Gs, with a few Fortresses from the USAAF winding up in Royal Canadian Air Force (RCAF) service during the war. To cope with increased demands for mail shipments to Canadian troops overseas, the RCAF formed No. 168 Squadron (Heavy Transport) in October 1943. USAAF chief Hap Arnold was sympathetic to Canadian requests for four-engine aircraft to carry morale-boosting mail overseas, and his interest in the Canadian request helped override U.S. Army objections as six B-17s were sold to Canada out of stateside training inventory. Three F-models received RCAF serials 9202 through 9204, and three B-17Es were given Canadian numbers 9205 through 9207. Some Canadians expressed concerns that the bombers they were sold were the dregs of the U.S. training fleet, but the RCAF made do with them. Canadian officials looked at the XC-108 transport modification of a B-17 as a possible model of conversion, but the immediate demand for mail planes saw the RCAF Fortresses enter service with minimal modifications at first.[1]

Loading and unloading of Canadian mail sacks often were through the radio room hatch. The mail-hauling Fortresses began service before Christmas 1943 and settled into

First foreign Fortresses and first in battle were former B-17Cs turned over to the Royal Air Force in 1941. Subsequently camouflaged, these Fortresses operated out of McChord Field near Tacoma, Washington, where British crews familiarized themselves with the Boeings before taking them back to England. *(Peter M. Bowers collection.)*

It was inevitable that some Fortresses in reasonable repair would fall into the hands of the Germans during the raging air war over Europe. B-17F 41-24585, a Seattle product, acquired Luftwaffe and Nazi markings in place of its former 303d Bomb Group identity and the American-applied nickname *Wulf Hound.* Captured in December 1942, the former *Wulf Hound* was pored over by German engineers, used as a flying teaching aid, evaluated at high altitude, and even used as a four-engine glider tug for the German DFS 230 program. By September 1943, this Fortress was passed on to a clandestine Luftwaffe unit, KG 200, where it probably received a nocturnal camouflage scheme to aid it in serving Germany on clandestine missions, as detailed in Hans-Heiri Stapfer's book, *Strangers in a Strange Land* published by Squadron/Signal Publications. *(Peter M. Bowers collection.)*

War booty, a captured early B-17E with remote belly turret, was given Japanese insignia and evaluated by that country. *(Peter M. Bowers collection.)*

their stride by January 1944. Test routes took them to the Middle East, Italy, and Gibraltar; regular service often terminated in Scotland or Gibraltar, with the mail offloaded there for its final destinations. The unarmed Canadian B-17s flew often at night, using cloud cover when possible to avoid detection by German fighters. Civilian passports were carried by the crew in the event of a forced landing in countries like Spain, Portugal, or Ireland to preclude international incidents. The B-17s of the RCAF crossed the Atlantic repeatedly between December 1943 and October 1944. Fortress number 9207 succumbed to a fatal crash at Prestwick in April 1944, possibly due to shifting cargo. Number 9204 was written off following a landing gear retraction on the ground at Rockliffe that September. On 15 December 1944, Fortress 9203 was lost somewhere between Morocco and the Azores; a few floating mailbags seemed to confirm its demise.

After the war, in October 1945, surviving RCAF B-17s rushed penicillin from Canada to Poland to meet an emergency humanitarian need. Fortress 9202 crashed in Germany in November 1945. When 168 Squadron was disbanded in March 1946, RCAF Fortress 9205 served on briefly as an air-sea rescue plane for No. 9 Group.[2]

Flying Fortress production never attained the quantities of B-24 Liberator output, and every B-17 produced had a ready home in the USAAF. Hence, few wartime foreign B-17s were in evidence.

Axis Fortresses

Germany was bound to inherit more-or-less intact B-17s as Fortresses came to earth on German-held territory. Some were test-flown in German markings and used to indoctrinate German fighter pilots; a few performed covert missions against the Allies while still wearing American stars. Other downed Fortresses were carted to the scrapper, yielding more aluminum for the German war machine.

Japan also tested a few captured B-17s, spoils from early Pacific victories. At least one appropriated B-17E was flown in Japanese markings for evaluation purposes.

There is some evidence to suggest the Soviet Air Force acquired a handful of B-17s including the possibility that the Soviets repaired Fortresses damaged by the Germans in a nocturnal bombing raid on Poltava, where USAAF B-17s gathered during a shuttle bombing mission.[3]

Some of the Flying Fortresses interned in neutral Sweden during the war, when they sought sanctuary there because of battle damage, were rebuilt and used as airliners in the immediate postwar years. This example, registered SE-BAK when it was operated by Swedish Airlines, featured extra fuselage windows and a curiously round-topped aft entry door. *(Bowers collection.)*

After World War II the fledgling Israeli Air Force launched an aircraft procurement campaign that netted a handful of tired-looking B-17Gs (see also Chapter 7).

The Dominican Republic gained a few armed B-17Gs, and Brazil used Fortresses for search and rescue missions long after the war. Sweden converted a number of B-17s into airliners, using aircraft that had diverted to that neutral country during bombing missions.

Notes

1. Carl Vincent, *Canada's Wings 2: The Liberator and Fortress,* Canada's Wings, Stittsville, Ontario, 1975.
2. *Ibid.*
3. Conversation, author with Ray Wagner, archivist, San Diego Aerospace Museum, 5 April 1999.

After Victory

B-17s in Postwar Use

Easy to fly and much beloved, the B-17 served the postwar U.S. Air Force, not as a bomber, but as a VIP transport as well as drone and drone director aircraft.

Hot Bikini

In July 1946, two atom bomb tests over Bikini atoll allowed the Air Force and other government agencies a systematic way to evaluate the destructive power and aftereffects of the new weapon less than a year after A-bombs heralded the abrupt end of World War II. The Bikini atoll tests represented only the fourth and fifth atomic bomb blasts ever. Unmanned Japanese and American ships were anchored off Bikini to bear witness to the atomic fury that would wash over them as a supersonic radioactive shock wave rolled out from the detonation point. Overhead, fleets of aircraft ranging from B-29s, C-54s, TBMs, F6F Hellcat fighters, and B-17s each had specific information-gathering duties.

B-17Gs used in Operation Crossroads over Bikini in 1946 operated out of Eniwetok. They included manned mother ships and remotely piloted drones fitted with cameras that could fly where men dared not go. Mechanical arms were clamped to the unique Fortress throttle grips and other control levers in the cockpits, responding to radio signals to change settings.

The blast detonated on Able Day, 1 July 1946, was attended by a total of nine B-17 mother ships and drones, orbiting at preassigned locations and altitudes overhead, using the call sign Marmalade. Cameras on the four drones performed their tasks well. Two Marmalade drone and control Fortresses circled about 12,500 ft overhead; another pair orbited at 18,000 ft; three more were staged at about 24,000 ft; and the last pair of B-17 drone and control aircraft were at nearly 30,000 ft when Test Able was detonated. The racetracks flown by the B-17s positioned them several miles out from the center of the blast.[1]

For Test Baker, on 25 July 1946, the first underwater nuclear detonation was made. A pair of Marmalade drone and control B-17Gs was stationed 6,000 ft above the ocean, with another pair about 1000 ft higher, while a single B-17, dubbed *Milkpail 9* (ASR patrol), flew

The end of the war in Europe saw some B-17s quickly stripped of heavy drag-producing turrets, as happened to this 305th Bomb Group example, possibly at Eschwege, Germany. Some Fortresses so lightened continued to serve in mapping and miscellaneous roles in Europe and North Africa; others flew home without the turrets. *(Fred LePage collection.)*

Most storied of several American surplus airfields after the war, Kingman, Arizona, received hundreds of combat-veteran B-17s that were scrapped there. If Americans have traditionally prided themselves in being courageous and innovative in wartime, it is another American trait to want to shed the military mantle as soon as peace is achieved. The treasures of Kingman went largely unappreciated except for a remarkable photo safari mounted by William T. Larkins, who is responsible for much of the Kingman photography extant. *(William T. Larkins photo via SDAM.)*

Boeing cleaned up a B-17G for use by Trans World Airlines in 1946 as a company airplane; everybody loved the Flying Fortress. *(Boeing via Peter M. Bowers.)*

Still chomping his cigar, Gen. Curtis LeMay observed a QB-17 drone ground controller during the 1946 Bikini nuclear Able and Baker tests. The Fortress drones could be manipulated from the ground or from a mother ship—another B-17—in flight. *(Air Force photo.)*

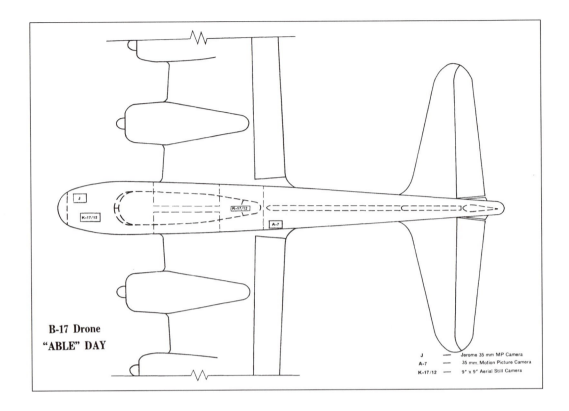

B-17 Drone
"ABLE" DAY

J	—	Jerome 35 mm MP Camera
A-7	—	35 mm. Motion Picture Camera
K-17/12	—	9" x 9" Aerial Still Camera

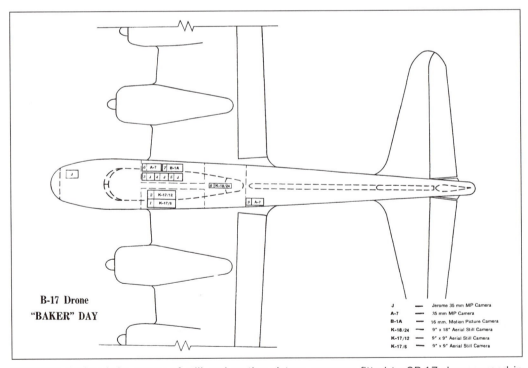

B-17 Drone
"BAKER" DAY

J	—	Jerome 35 mm MP Camera
A-7	—	35 mm MP Camera
B-1A	—	16 mm. Motion Picture Camera
K-18/24	—	9" x 18" Aerial Still Camera
K-17/12	—	9" x 9" Aerial Still Camera
K-17/6	—	9" x 9" Aerial Still Camera

Diagrams depicted the arrays of still and motion-picture cameras fitted to QB-17 drones used in Able and Baker Day nuclear tests at Bikini in 1946. The use of unmanned B-17s allowed the collection of nuclear blast photography from altitudes and distances considered dangerous to humans.

at about 6500 ft. Among the F6Fs, TBMs, and PBMs, another pair of Marmalade B-17 drone and control Fortresses loitered at 11,000 ft, topped by still another pair at 16,000 ft, with the solo Marmalade master drone controller B-17G aloft at 18,000 ft.[2]

Even the mother ship Fortresses over Bikini carried cameras, ranging from 16-mm and 35-mm movie installations to 5 in by 5 in K-24/20 aerial cameras. For Able Day, the B-17G drones carried a large 9 in by 9 in aerial still camera in the nose and amidships, as well as 35-mm movie cameras in the nose and amidships. More elaborate was the Baker Day Fortress drone camera configuration, with the bomb bay hosting duplicate 9 in by 9 in still cameras and an array of 35-mm motion picture cameras, plus a K-18/24 9 in by 18 in still camera amidships and other movie cameras amidships and in the nose.

A contemporary narrative described the B-17 drones' activities: "The crewless drones, B-17 Flying Fortresses, carried many cameras into the atomic cloud on Able Day. A still camera and a motion picture camera (K-17, Jerome B-2) shot forward from each plane, while another still camera (K-17) took vertical views. Each radar altimeter was photographed by a motion picture camera (modified A-7)." The Jerome and K-17 cameras were operated simultaneously in each of the drone B-17s when activated by the mother ships. A clock was set in motion when the cameras started, and it ran for a predetermined length of time before automatically sending a signal through the control panel that shut off power to all of the cameras.[3]

For Baker Day, only one of the drones aloft carried cameras other than those used to record the radar altimeter readings. All cameras on this Fortress were mounted vertically, with the focal-lengths of still-camera lenses varying between 6 and 24 in. A report on the Bikini tests said: "This aircraft was over the target array at the time of detonation and obtained some very excellent pictures."[4]

The drone B-17Gs of Bikini had a few more tricks after Able and Baker Days in July 1946. A mother-and-drone pair flew from Hawaii to Muroc Army Air Base in California to tout the drones' long-range capabilities, and for the 1949 motion picture *Twelve O'clock High,* several of the Crossroads QB-17Gs were flown. In 1958, a Crossroads-veteran mother ship, DB-17 number 44-85738, was ferried to the agrarian town of Tulare, in California's San Joaquin Valley, for permanent display as a war memorial.

Like its manned wartime counterparts, this QB-17 target drone at Holloman Air Force Base, New Mexico, was landed in spite of substantial damage to its tail section in June 1952. *(Air Force photo.)*

A grand lineup of Boeing heavyweights photographed at Boeing Field in July 1956 included an Air Force VIP B-17G followed by a B-29, B-47, C-97, and B-52. If the B-17 put Boeing on the map, the company did not rest on its laurels, but innovated its way into the future once victory was achieved in World War II. *(Boeing photo.)*

To Israel

The fledgling Israeli state in 1948 perceived an immediate need to equip an air force. To that end, a number of B-17Gs in civilian ownership in the United States were bought and transferred to Israel. At least four Fortresses at one time listed as belonging to A. Schwimmer of Miami, Florida, subsequently flew the Atlantic toward Israel; one (44-83842, U.S. registration NL 1212N) reportedly was impounded by Portugal at the Azores in July 1948 and subsequently used by the Portuguese Air Force. Another, 44-83811, evidently served Israel for a decade beginning in 1948. When it was dismantled in Israel in 1958, its fuselage survived to be shipped to England in 1961 for use in the stark black-and-white war film, *The War Lover,* after which it was scrapped at a Middlesex salvage yard. G-model number 44-83753 lasted about 10 years before meeting the scrapper in Israel; 44-83851 was said to be salvaged in Israel by about 1962.[5]

Some of the Israeli Fortresses received a multicolored desert camouflage scheme surmounted by white-disked blue stars of David, the traditional Israeli Air Force insignia. Photos show machine guns mounted in open waist windows, but no power turrets fitted.

At least one of the Israeli B-17Gs, former U.S. civil registration number NL-5024N, had entered the civilian marketplace at Altus, Oklahoma, in August 1947. Altus

The sound of whispering R-1820s on short final approach heralded the arrival of Arnold Kolb flying one of his B-17 firebombers at Coeur d'Alene, Idaho, in August 1973. Kolb's Black Hills Aviation operated several B-17s over the years; this example later became part of the Smithsonian Institution's National Air and Space Museum collection. *(Photo by Frederick A. Johnsen.)*

Following a stint as a war memorial in the unusually named Stuttgart, Arkansas, this B-17F, some-times nicknamed *Great White Bird,* was acquired by Max Biegert who dismantled it to move it to the airport for reassembly and flight in the early 1950s. After about three decades of use as a fire-bomber, fire-ant poisoner, and sometimes movie star, this Fortress was rebuilt and restored for the Museum of Flight in Seattle, Washington. *(Max Biegert collection.)*

was a storage and disposition airfield for surplus planes. NL-5024N was stripped of its military hardware in Oklahoma to better suit it for civilian use. While the presence of military gear might have heightened the Fortress's use to the Israeli Air Force, the absence of it made it easier for the more benign-looking civil-registered aircraft to make its way out of the United States and over to the Middle East without arousing suspicions of the countries along the flight path of the B-17.[6]

Where's the Fire?

The availability of a variety of surplus aircraft with bomb bays—and a few without—gave rise to a host of firefighting aircraft that could tank thousands of gallons of fire retardant over remote and sometimes impassable wilderness, dropping the liquid in a systematic way to contain the spread of flames. State and federal agencies were willing to pay for such services, making practical the nomadic life of the borate bomber. (Borate was an early chemical retardant added to water, and the alliterative moniker "borate bomber" outlived the actual use of borate, as firefighters switched to a phosphate-based chemical that actually fertilizes the charred ground to promote rapid regrowth of vegetation.)

Aerial firefighting was a mixed blessing for postwar B-17s. While most of the surviving examples of Fortresses at one time stayed viable as fire bombers, the risky business also claimed a number of B-17s in accidents. Surplus B-17s, ranging from ex-Navy PB-1Ws to former trade-school and city-park veterans, were modified with boxy tanks shoehorned into the bomb bay.

Registered N17W, the former *Great White Bird* sprayed poison to combat gypsy moths in downtown Lansing, Michigan, in 1953. Because the fuselage cross section at the nose is the same for B-17Es through Gs, surviving F-models in postwar civilian use often used readily available B-17G Plexiglas nose caps. *(Dick Baxter via Boeing.)*

The U.S. Navy initiated work on getting its own B-17s during the war when radar-equipped pickets were needed to warn the U.S. Fleet of Japanese intentions. Not available in time for combat, the Navy's sea blue PB-1W Fortresses served into the 1950s. *(Gordon S. Williams collection.)*

The roster of firefighting B-17s includes:

B-17F-BO 42-29782, registration N17W, air tanker numbers E84, C44, and O4; purchased by Bob Richardson and saved for the Museum of Flight, Seattle, Washington.

B-17F-VE 42-6107, N1340N, operated variously as tanker 35, 34, and A34; converted to take Rolls Royce Dart turboprop engines circa 1970 by Aero Flite of Cody, Wyoming; crashed in August 1970 while fighting fires in Wyoming.

B-17G 42-102715, N66573, operated as tanker E85, A10, and 10; crashed fighting fires in Montana in 1979; scalloped paint gave rise to nickname *Batmobile.*

B-17G 44-85774, N621L, tanker C64, 64; crashed July 1975.

B-17G-VE 44-85778, N3509G, tanker E16, 42, 102; to Bob Pond for flying display.

B-17G-VE 44-85813, N6694C, tanker C12 (former five-engine testbed); crashed fighting fires, Bear Pen, North Carolina, 1980.

B-17G-VE 44-85828, N9323R, tanker 30 and 37; retired to Pima Air Museum, Tucson, Arizona, by the 1980s.

B-17G-VE 44-85829, N3193G, tanker numbers C34 and 34; sold to "Yankee Air Force" for preservation and display beginning in 1986.

B-17G-VE 44-85840, N620L, tanker number C54; crashed near Elko, Nevada, while fire bombing, July 1973.

B-17G 43-38635, N3702G, tanker E61, 61; retired to Castle Air Museum, Atwater, California, 1979.

B-17G-DL 44-83514, N9323Z, early fire bomber conversion, circa 1959 by Aero Union, tanker numbers E17, 17; acquired by "Confederate Air Force" for displays beginning in 1978 as *Sentimental Journey.*

B-17G-DL 44-83542, N9324Z, air tanker numbers E18, 18; crashed fighting fires in July 1971; parts saved for other restorations.

B-17G-DL 44-83546, N3703G, air tanker E78, E68, 68; acquired by Military Aircraft Restoration Group in 1982; flown by David Tallichet to represent title aircraft for 1990 film, *Memphis Belle.*

B-17G-DL 44-83563, N9563Z, veteran of movie, *The War Lover;* subsequently tanker numbers C24, 89; acquired by National Warplane Museum, Geneseo, New York, in 1986.

B-17G-DL 44-83575, N93012, survivor of Nevada atomic testing in 1952, sufficiently "cool" to be sold for scrap in 1965; ferried off test site in 1965; stored in Mesa, Arizona, until brought into tanker use by 1977; tanker number 99; auctioned in 1985 to become flying display replicating Eighth Air Force B-17G *Nine-O-Nine.*

B-17G-DL 44-83785, N809Z and N207EV, tanker numbers C71, 71, 22; restored for display by Evergreen Aviation beginning in the mid-1980s.

B-17G-DL 44-83814, N66571, tanker A18, 09; to National Air and Space Museum ownership by 1981.

B-17G-DL 44-83863, N5233V, tanker 71, D1, 18; to USAF Armament Museum at Eglin Air Force Base, Florida, by 1975.

B-17G-DL 44-83864, N73648, tanker B11; crashed 1972.

B-17G-DL 44-83868, N5237V, tanker 15, 65; to Great Britain for RAF Museum by 1983.

B-17G-DL 44-83884, N5230V, Aero Union tanker numbers C19, 19; to Eighth Air Force Museum for display at Barksdale Air Force Base, Louisiana, by 1978.[7]

The first Fortress to be preserved expressly as a flying display was the G-model nicknamed *Texas Raiders* by a group of aviation enthusiasts who gathered in Texas under the moniker, Confederate Air Force. The aircraft was given U.S. civil registration number N7227C. Since this 1976 photograph, the long-lived aircraft received a makeover including the addition of turrets and new paint. *(Author photo.)*

The spectacle of two B-17s in military markings in formation, one streaming special-effects smoke, was part of the Confederate Air Force air demonstration held in the south Texas town of Harlingen in October 1977. *(Photo by Frederick A. Johnsen.)*

The enterprise of American fliers is not to be underestimated. Arnold Kolb, whose Black Hills Aviation operated three B-17 fire bombers for years, used the open-air ramp space at his Spearfish, South Dakota, base to graft the complete nose section of one B-17G onto another to make a viable fire bomber. The recipient of the new front end was the former engine testbed Fortress used by Curtiss-Wright (B-17G number 44-85813), which had been radically shortened to take a new nose that could mount a fifth engine for flight testing. The donor was a fuselage (B-17G number 44-83316) that had been used as back lot dressing for the *12 O'clock High* television series in the 1960s. As Kolb and his crew labored in 1969–1970 to splice the nose onto their unusual Fortress, the warming rays of the sun posed alignment problems as the sunny side of the B-17 expanded more than the side in shadows. But ingenuity—and plumb bobs—prevailed, and the Fortress was eventually aligned and assembled.[8]

The resulting stock-looking B-17 obtained Restricted category certification in December 1970 and served as a fire bomber, carrying two 1200-gal retardant tanks in the bomb bay. Registered as N6694C, Kolb's rebuilt air tanker fought fires around the United States until 1980, when it crashed at the picturesque-sounding Bear Pen airport in North Carolina. The forward fuselage that Kolb had so carefully attached burned up. Other remnants of the airframe were subsequently shipped to Florida awaiting possibly yet another resurrection with parts from other Fortresses.[9]

Visitors to the Strategic Aerospace Museum near Omaha, Nebraska, in 1980 inspected a former drone-director B-17G, dwarfed by the gargantuan Cold War Convair B-36 Peacemaker looming behind it. *(Photo by Frederick A. Johnsen.)*

With a skilled pilot at the controls, the B-17 could be taxied on its main wheels, as the G-model called *Sentimental Journey* showed at the Paine Field, Washington, air show in the summer of 1979. *(Photo by Frederick A. Johnsen.)*

Starting in the late 1940s, a surplus B-17G presided over sales of gasoline in the Portland suburb of Milwaukie, Oregon. *(Herb Tollefson photo.)*

Restored from a cut and modified hulk, the wartime survivor 91st Bomb Group's *Shoo Shoo Shoo Baby* was rebuilt by volunteers at Dover Air Force Base, Delaware, between 1978 and 1988, when it was triumphantly flown to the Air Force Museum in Dayton, Ohio, for permanent display. *(Courtesy Mike Leister.)*

Notes

1. *Official Report—Operation Crossroads,* by Task Unit 1.52 (undated, circa August–September 1946).
2. *Ibid.*
3. *Ibid.*
4. *Ibid.*
5. John Chapman and Geoff Goodall, *Warbirds Worldwide Directory,* Warbirds Worldwide Ltd., Mansfield, England, 1989.
6. "Saga of the Civil Forts," James H. Farmer, *American Aviation Historical Society Journal,* Vol. 22, No. 4, Winter 1977.
7. *Ibid.*
8. From discussions between the author and Arnold Kolb, 1973–1974.
9. Scott A. Thompson, *Final Cut—The Post-War B-17 Flying Fortress: The Survivors,* Pictorial Histories Publishing Co., Missoula, Mont., 1990.

Appendix
Representative Flying Fortress Specifications

Model	Length	Span	Gross wt, lb	Cruise speed, mi/h	Top speed, mi/h
Y1B-17	68′ 4″	103′ 9″	42,600	217	256
B-17C	67′ 11″	103′ 9″	46,650	231	291
B-17E	73′ 10″	103′ 9″	53,000	210	317
B-17F	74′ 9″	103′ 9″	55,000*	200	299
B-17G	74′ 4″	103′ 9″	65,500	182	287
XB-38	74′	103′ 9″	56,000**	226	327

*Maximum weight, 65,500 lb

**Maximum weight, 64,000 lb

Aircraft statistics are subject to variables; these numbers provide a trend in Fortress performance, although different tables sometimes tally different weight and speed numbers. Altitude champion was the F-model, with a service ceiling of 37,500 ft. One remarkable constant throughout B-17 production is the broad wing design, which evolved but not radically. At an empty weight of over 36,135 lb, the wartime B-17G was almost 6 tons heavier than the empty weight of the Y1B-17.

12 O'Clock High television series, 151

Ackerman, First Lt. Clifton, 91–93

Air Corps Tactical School, 2, 3

Alkire, Captain Darr H., 9

Andrews, Maj. Gen. Frank M., 9

Anzio, 95

Arnold, Gen. Henry H. (Hap), 4, 7, 56, 60, 61, 70, 74, 76, 85, 94, 137

Aircraft, Germany:

  FW-190, 57, 61, 76, 108

  Me-163, 108

  Me-262, 80, 97, 108

  V-1 (buzz bomb), 91, 108

Aircraft, Great Britain:

  DB-7B, 137

  Fortress I, 11

  Spitfire, 56, 57

Aircraft, Japan, Nakajima Hayabusa ("Oscar"), 53, 54

Aircraft, United States:

  A-20, 137

  B-17B, 18, 19

  B-17C, 11, 19, 20, 137, 155

  B-17D, 18, 20, 47, 51, 117, 135

  B-17E, 20, 21, 27, 28, 33, 34, 51, 55–58, 62, 117–119, 123, 131, 135, 137, 139, 155

  B-17F, 21, 22, 28, 30–32, 37–40, 42, 58, 59, 62, 109, 111, 113, 125, 126, 130, 131, 133, 135, 137, 149, 155

  B-17G, 22, 24, 26–28, 30, 32, 33, 55, 60, 62, 107, 114, 122, 126, 130–133, 135–137, 140, 141, 145, 146, 149, 151, 155

  B-17H, 27, 55

  B-18, 4, 51

B-24, 28, 33, 50, 51, 52, 53, 55, 58, 60–62, 65, 69, 72, 74, 80, 82–86, 88, 95, 97, 101, 118, 121, 130, 132, 137, 139

B-24D, 30, 58, 59, 61, 126

B-25, 52, 95, 113, 114, 126, 130

B-26, 95

B-29, 37, 52, 74, 141

B-40, 29, 31

BT-13, 114

BQ-7, 27

C-46, 33

C-54, 141

C-108, 27

C-109, 28

Curtiss Jenny, 1

DB-17, 145

DC-3, 17

F-4, 28

F-5, 28

F6F, 141, 145

F-7, 28

F-9, 28

FB-17, 28

Model 80, 34

Model 247, 15, 34

Model 299, 3, 7, 15–17, 117, 133

Model 314, 15, 33

P-38, 28, 29, 55, 69, 83, 84, 97

P-39, 29, 106

P-40, 29

P-47, 76, 81, 93, 111

P-51, 32, 84, 85, 91, 92, 93

P-63, 29

PB-1W, 147

PBM, 145

QB-17, 27, 145

RB-17G, 28

SB-17, 27, 55

SBD Dauntless, 51, 52

TBM, 141, 145

UC-78, 114

XB-15, 15, 16, 33

XB-38, 28, 29, 155

XB-41, 30

Y1B-17, 4–8, 15–17, 155

Y1B-17A, 18

YB-17, 17

YB-40, 30, 32, 33, 126

YC-108, 28

Bad Penny, 107, 114

Bastille Day, 108

Batmobile, 149

Beall, Wellwood, 33

Bendix chin turret, 30, 32, 126, 131

Big Week, 85

Bikini atoll, 141, 145

Boeing, 22, 26

Boeing Field, 6

Berlin, 68, 74, 84–86, 97, 114, 115

Bowman, SSgt. Richard E., 105–109

Brereton, Gen., 51, 55

Brower, Lt. Col. G. E., 4, 5

Buck, Dr. J. H., 73

Buenos Aires, 8

Cheyenne tail gun emplacement, 135, 136

Cheyenne, Wyoming, 30

Clark Field, Philippines, 48

Cole, Jerry, 109–113

Combined bomber offensive (CBO), 65

Congress, United States, 6
Corkille, Maj. John, 17

Davis, Capt. S. O., 44
Devers, General J. L., 76
Dieppe, 57
Doolittle, Lt. Gen. Jimmy, 84, 85, 101
Douglas, 21, 22, 26

Eagle radar, 68, 73, 74
Eaker, Maj. Gen. Ira, 58, 65, 69, 70, 72
Eisenhower, Gen. Dwight D., 88
Engines, aircraft:
    Allison V-1710-89 engine, 28
    Pratt and Whitney R-1690 Hornet, 16, 17
    Wright R-1820 Cyclone, 17, 19, 20, 37, 39

Five Grand, 109
Fort Lewis, Washington, 65
Frugone, Capt. Attilio, 10

Gee, 65
Geiger Field, Washington, 109
Giles, Gen. Barney, 74
Goddard, Maj. George, 10
Green, SSgt. James, 62
Grenier Field, New Hampshire, 68
Guadalcanal, 52

H2S radar, 65, 68–70
H2X radar, 68–74
Hallion, Richard P., 76
Halverson, Col. Harry, 55
Hamilton-Standard propellers, 16, 37
Hansell, Brig. Gen. Haywood, 31
Haynes, Maj. Caleb V., 9
Hiryu aircraft carrier, 52

Israeli Air Force, 140, 146

Kasserine Pass, 83
Kearney Army Airfield, Nebraska, 107
Kelly, Capt. Colin P. Jr., 48
Kenney, Gen. George, 53
Kolb, Arnold, 151

Lackland Air Force Base, Texas, 114
Langley Field, Virginia, 6, 8, 9
LeMay, Gen. Curtis, 3, 6, 9, 10, 78, 80, 82, 117
Lindbergh, Charles, 60

Lockheed, 21
Lowry Field, Colorado, 109

MacArthur, Gen. Douglas, 3, 51
March Field, California, 7, 9
Marcilonis, SSgt., Ben, 62
Maxwell Field, Alabama, 9
Meloy, Maj. V. J., 10
Memphis Belle, 58
Memphis Belle film, 149
Merrill, A. Elliott, 37–40
Messe, Marshall, 83
MGM, 9
Midway Island, 51, 52
Mirgorod, 91, 93
Mitchell, Brig. Gen. Billy, 1, 2
Mitchel Field, New York, 10
Monte Cassino, 95
Muroc Army Air Base, California, 6
My Gal Sal, 58

National Advisory Committee for Aeronautics (NACA), 9, 20, 37
National Broadcasting Corporation, 10
Nichols Field, 51
Nine-o-nine, 149
Norden bombsight, 3, 114
Normandy, 72

Oboe, 65, 68, 70
Olds, Lt. Col. Robert, 6, 8, 9
Operation Argument, 84, 85
Operation Bolero, 58–60
Operation Cadillac Series Three, 108
Operation Chow Hound, 97
Operation Crossroads, 141, 145
Operation Market Garden, 109
Operation Starkey, 80
Operation Torch, 60, 61
Ortiz, Roberto M., 8

Pathfinders, 68, 69
Peenemunde, 115
Pershing, Gen. John J., 1
Ploesti, 95, 97
Poltava, 91–93, 107, 139
Portuguese Air Force, 146
Pratt, Adm. William V., 3
Punitive expedition into Mexico, 1
Pyote, Texas, 106–107

Randolph Field, Texas, 9
Reid, Col. William, 32
Regensburg, 78, 80
Rex Italian ocean liner, 9, 10

Rommel, Gen. Erwin, 55, 83
Royal Air Force, 11, 56, 57, 65, 68, 85
Royal Canadian Air Force (RCAF), 137, 139
Royal Flying Corps, 1

Seattle, Washington, 7
Schweinfurt, 78, 80, 81
Sentimental Journey, 149
Sicily, 83
Soviet Air Force, 139
Spaatz, Gen. Carl, 55, 60, 61, 85, 88, 94
Sperry ball turret, 21, 106–108, 110–112, 118, 119
Sperry remote ventral turret, 117–119
Sperry upper turret, 39, 123, 131
Sweeney, Lt. Col. Walter C., 49, 50

Tacoma, Washington, 37, 39
Test Pilot, film, 9
Test, Roy, 113–115
Tobruk, 55
Tokyo tanks, 38
Tower, Les, 7
Trenchard, Maj. Gen. Hugh M., 1
Twelve O'Clock High motion picture, 145
Tyndall Field, Florida, 105, 106, 109

U-boats, 61, 62, 65, 68, 84
Umstead, Capt. Stanley, 6, 17
United Airlines modification center, Cheyenne, Wyoming, 135
United States Army Air Forces, units
    11th Bomb Group, 51, 52
    19th Bomb Group, 47, 51
    20th Bomb Squadron, 8
    43d Bomb Group, 52–54
    49th Bomb Squadron, 9
    90th Bomb Group, 52, 53
    91st Bomb Group, 62
    92d Bomb Group, 31–32, 57
    93d Bomb Group, 61
    96th Bombardment Squadron, 9
    96th Bomb Group, 107–109
    97th Bomb Group, 55, 61, 83, 84, 91, 92
    99th Bomb Group, 83, 84
    100th Bomb Group, 86
    301st Bomb Group, 55, 83, 84
    303d Bomb Group, 31, 62
    305th Bomb Group, 6, 62, 83, 117
    306th Bomb Group, 62
    375th Troop Carrier Group, 54
    379th Bomb Group, 31

388th Bomb Group, 81
390th Bomb Group, 109, 110, 112, 113
398th Bomb Group, 114
433d Troop Carrier Group, 54
463d Bomb Group, 84
482d Bomb Group, 68, 71, 73

483d Bomb Group, 84
Fifth Bomb Group, 51, 52
First Bombardment Wing, 31
First Provisional Group, 55
Second Bomb Group, 6, 9, 83, 84

Vega, 21, 22, 26, 27

Wait, Louis, 7
Wake Island, 51
War Department, 2, 3, 6, 55
(The) War Lover film, 146, 149
West, Sgt. Kent R., 57
Wilhelmshaven, 11
Wright Field, Ohio, 7, 9

Frederick A. Johnsen is one of the world's foremost authorities on U.S. military aviation history and the author of more than 15 books on the subject. An Air Force historian since 1981, he was formerly a consulting curator for an aerospace museum, and editor of *Western Flyer*. His books include *B-24 Liberator: Rugged but Right, P-47 Thunderbolt, A-26 Invader, F4U Corsair,* and *Douglas A-1 Skyraider*. He has contributed to many aviation and general interest periodicals, including *Aviation Week and Space Technology, FlyPast,* and the *Seattle Times*. Assigned to the Flight Test Center at Edwards Air Force Base, he has been a collector of flight memorabilia since the age of 5 in 1956.